Daydreamer

© 2022 Mike Trial

All rights reserved. No part of this book may be reproduced or transmitted in any form or by any means, electronic or mechanical or by any information or storage and retrieval system without permission in writing from the author or publisher.

Published by
Compass Flower Press

ISBN 978-1-951960-41-4

Daydreamer

Mike Trial

Prologue

I was eight years old when we returned to Kansas City.

Even though I was born there I had no memory of it since my parents and I had been living overseas from the time I was three years old. My father, George Trial, had been stationed at Dhahran Air Base, Saudi Arabia, while he was on active duty with the US Air Force. In March 1949, when family housing became available, my mother, Ruth, joined him there, bringing me, age three, with her. In March 1950 my father left the Air Force and went to work for the oil company ARAMCO, also in Dhahran. My sister Linden and I grew up in the comfortable ARAMCO housing compound at Dhahran.

But in the summer of 1954, my parents became increasingly concerned about the declining health of my grandmother Juna (my mother's mother). My aunt Bonnie was caring for Juna and teaching school full time, which was becoming too much for her. My parents decided that my mother, with my sister and me, would live in Kansas City to help care for Juna, while my father returned alone to his job in Dhahran.

So in the summer of 1954, my parents, my sister, and I travelled east from Saudi Arabia through Asia, across the Pacific and onward to Kansas City, arriving in late August. In early September my mother, my sister, and I moved into rented rooms in a house in Kansas City near where my grandmother and aunt Bonnie lived. My father returned to Dhahran.

This reminiscence covers the period from August 1954 through June 1957. It is based on the neatly labeled photos my father took of these long-ago events, a few diary entries, some souvenirs, and my own recollections. For periods where there were no photos, I have added interpolations as to what probably occurred.

Kansas City 1954

The TWA DC-7 circled once over downtown Kansas City then settled to a smooth landing. The five of us—my father, my mother, my aunt, my sister, and I—gathered up our things and walked across the tarmac to the terminal in 101-degree heat. It was five PM, August 27, 1954. After collecting our voluminous luggage, we piled into two taxis and rode to 4410 Garfield Avenue, my grandmother's house.

While my parents opened suitcases and made sleeping arrangements for us, I wandered down Garfield Avenue. It was a quiet residential street in what was at the time a solidly middle-class neighborhood. The temperature was cooling as the sun sank, and it was comfortable in the shade of the big elm and oak trees that lined the street. The sidewalk was cracked and buckled in places by tree roots. Cicadas droned. The houses seemed very close together, not more than ten feet between them. They were very similar wooden frame, with aged paint. Most had porches with two-person swings suspended on chains from the porch ceiling.

A few people were slowly rocking in their gliders, the men mostly reading the newspaper, the women fanning themselves with paper fans. "Hello young man," a bald-headed man wearing an undershirt called cheerfully.

"Hello," I said tentatively, moving along.

"Hot ain't it?"

"Yes, sir," I told him, thinking it was cooler than Dhahran.

He went back to reading the *Kansas City Star*.

I walked north on Garfield avenue then right on 44th Street, right on Park Avenue to 45th Street, then back to 4410 Garfield. There was no traffic on these streets but I could hear the cars on The Paseo, only six blocks away. It was almost dark by the time I climbed the steps to my grandmother's front porch. She had a two-person swing on the porch which I resolved to try out tomorrow. The house seemed small and dark inside compared to our roomy (and air conditioned) concrete block house in Dhahran. The wooden floor at the place where the dining room and living room joined had a creak in it, which I worked in a sort of free form melody until my father told me to quit doing that.

Our luggage, all eight suitcases, was stacked in the corner of the dining room. Sheets and blankets had been laid out on the sofa and on the floor of the living room. Even though there was no air conditioning, the rooms were cool, lit only by a single light fixture in the middle of the ceiling of each room. We ate a hasty dinner off paper plates and soon afterward I fell into a deep sleep in my sleeping bag on the living room floor. The soft hum of an oscillating fan reminded me of the air conditioning at our house in Dhahran.

The next day I wandered the neighborhood again, in the humid Missouri morning. I tested the swing on the porch until my grandmother told me I was swinging too high. About noon my uncle Jack and aunt Doris arrived by train from their home in Superior, Wisconsin. They brought with them a bottle of champagne as a welcome-home gift for my parents. Uncle Jack, a round faced, jovial man, always the center of attention, officiated with a toast and many jokes. My sister and I had ginger ale—Canada Dry— which I love to this day. Uncle Jack's jokes and the champagne had everyone laughing uproariously, even my grandmother Juna.

My uncle Jack and aunt Doris visited us in Missouri each summer while I was in high school and college. They were happy people who enjoyed golf and fishing. Every visit, uncle Jack and I would tromp through the weeds to a pond on the farm and fish for bluegill. We usually caught many (the pond was overstocked) and spent far too much time cleaning miniscule fish to get one bite filets. But they tasted good fried over an open fire as the sun set. I never met a more congenial person than Uncle Jack. He and his wife Doris were inseparable. They both died in the 1980s and are buried together in a quiet cemetery in Superior, Wisconsin. I miss them.

    While adults all chatted in the stuffy living room I went out exploring again. In those days it was perfectly safe for kids to walk alone in that part of town. I ran my fingers over the rough bark of the big old elm trees and stared up at their tops swaying in the humid breeze. Blue jays called from a distance, which seemed a very melancholy sound to me. I was surprised at how hilly it was. There were narrow alleys behind the houses lined with one-car garages just barely big enough for a car. Many, but not all families, had cars. My grandmother still had her deceased husband Mack's car, which neither she nor Bonnie drove very often. In those days you could get around Kansas City easily on buses and streetcars. Cars were for longer trips. The Troost Avenue streetcar was very convenient for trips to the Plaza or to downtown. And like most neighborhoods, there was a tiny grocery store two blocks away from my grandmother's house that stocked daily-use foodstuffs like fresh milk, eggs, and Wonder bread in its white wrapper with blue and red polka dots.

    The next day my father took the car and drove two hours to Effingham, Kansas, to visit his mother, Grace. She was a widow and lived by herself on a twenty-acre farm.

    My grandmother Juna kept to her bedroom most of the day. My mother spent the day organizing our luggage and caring for her mother while Bonnie was at Westwood View School teaching fourth grade. I wandered the streets.

    My father returned that night and told us that his mother was fine. Effingham was a tiny farm community in eastern Kansas. My father told me she wanted to see all of us and maybe we could go for a visit sometime this year.

    The next day my mother and father started looking for a nearby place to rent for a year, and soon found one at 5720 Virginia Avenue. The woman who owned the house, Mrs. Walker, lived with her three kids on the ground floor and rented out the top floor, which consisted of three small bedrooms, a bathroom, and a tiny sitting room.

We moved in. Renters had permission to use the kitchen on the ground floor, and my mother quickly became good friends with Mrs. Walker. They spent many hours sitting drinking coffee and talking at the kitchen table.

And it was only four blocks away from my grandmother's house. There was no air conditioning and I don't remember ever missing it, although our house in Dhahran had central air conditioning.

My mother enrolled me in the third grade at Troost School, an elementary school four blocks away. My sister, only four years old, stayed with my mother as she cared for Grandmother Juna. The school building was the standard 1950s three-story brick schoolhouse, with echoing stairways and a bare asphalt playground fenced with a ten-foot-high chain-link fence. It seemed fine to me. I have no memories of any of my classes, my teachers, or other kids in the school, with one exception. I got to know a kid named Kurt who was the same age as me. His mother and my mother were both in PTA, and sometimes Kurt would come to my house after school and sometimes I'd go to his.

One thing I remember vividly about my first days at Troost School was a yellow cocker spaniel on the route I walked to and from school. I dreaded seeing the dog in the yard because as soon as he spotted me walking along the sidewalk, he would run at me, barking ferociously. Fortunately he stopped at the edge of his owner's lawn. I soon began crossing the street to avoid the dog, and later walking one block away, until I was safely past that house. I've never liked dogs ever since those days. Thankfully cold weather came soon, the dog was kept in the house, and I could resume walking straight down the block.

My sister and I soon got to know the Walker kids pretty well. There were three of them: James, the oldest, a heavy-set kid with dark hair. Tommy, who was my age, was a sandy-haired, spindly boy with high shoulders. He did not resemble James at all, but he and his five-year-old sister were clearly related. Although James was a year older than me, I found myself hanging around with him more than with Tommy. James had the same vivid imagination I did and liked to tell stories, just like I did. So we'd often wander the neighborhood after school telling each other adventure stories that were partly what we'd seen at the movies or read in comic books, but were mostly made up.

Not long after we'd moved into the upstairs rooms at the Walker house, my father told my sister and me that he had to go back to work. And since his work was back in Dhahran, Saudi Arabia, that meant he'd be away for several months. "But I'll be back my next vacation."

And somehow it wasn't an overwhelmingly emotional event when he left. My mother and father always kept a confident and positive attitude in front of us, so my sister and I never had any doubt that things would be fine, that he would come back and things would be just the same as always.

As I think back to those days, I now appreciate how my parents never let my sister and me feel any doubt that our family was safe and secure. We moved many times while I was a kid, but our family remained the same—stable and loving.

I seldom thought about Dhahran, where I'd lived until now. It had been home, but now Kansas City was home. Once in a while I'd think about red-haired Jim McGruder, my best friend, who lived four houses away in Dhahran. We used to set up elaborate river systems in the back yard of my house by running the hose through the sandy soil and patchy grass. It was pleasant under the acacia tree, which also was our climbing tree. Although it was short, it had a nice bough about five feet off the ground, perfect for climbing. As we constructed our river landscape we would invent characters and adventures and act them out in a play that combined model cars and trucks, the tree, and the tiny river system. It was great fun.

When I was about six years old I learned to ride a bike on the street behind our house in Dhahran. My father bought me a small bike (the kind where the pedals go around any time the rear wheel is turning, which was a problem, as were the solid rubber tires that made for a jolting ride). After a few falls I got the knack and then pedaled up and down the street behind our house endlessly. Soon my parents bought me a bigger and better bike (with air-filled tires) and allowed me to pedal all around the blocks near our house. It was a housing compound, so there was almost no traffic during the day. Such a sense of freedom and power! Before I got my bike I had walked to school and to the swimming pool, the theater and the library, but now I could cover those three or four blocks in no time, riding along with the hot breeze flowing past. It was wonderful.

Strangely, while we lived in Kansas City, I didn't have a bike, and I don't remember wanting one. Kids are flexible and adaptable.

Cooler days came, bringing an occasional cold rain. Walking home from school, I delayed to look closely at the red and yellow oak leaves lying on the sidewalk. At night I would sometimes leave my bedroom window open just a crack to let cold air flow into the room, while I lay warm and cozy under my blankets; so different from the desert heat of Dhahran.

One rainy afternoon after school I strolled up and down the sidewalk in my raincoat and rubber boots, pretending I was a giant robot, stamping through the water running down toward the storm drains carrying red and gold leaves. Wandering around, comfortable in boots and raincoat while rain misted down, was great fun. Back home Mrs. Walker or my mother would often have chocolate chip cookies on a plate. We were limited to two cookies each.

One cool, clear autumn Saturday my mother took my sister and me downtown with her while she did some shopping. The streetcars ran on Troost Avenue in steel tracks with roof-mounted flexible rods that slid along overhead power lines. Mother, with my sister and me in tow, would shop at The Jones Store, or Emery, Bird, Thayer, or Macy's, which were block-long, multi-floor, full-service department stores in those days, with elevators and elevator operators in uniforms. It was fun traipsing around the aisles full of clothing, jewelry, or household goods. This trip my mother bought a box of Russell Stover raspberry parfaits, and I ate four of them while we waited for the streetcar home. About halfway home, with the motion of the streetcar, the crowded seats and aisle, the too-bright afternoon sun, I started feeling queasy, but I made it home. No more raspberry parfaits for a while.

My mother enrolled me in Cub Scouts for a time. It was not anything I really wanted to do, and I found I didn't enjoy it much. I have no memories of any of the activities, except once we were to learn to tie certain kinds of knots, which I never did master. After a few weeks my mother relented, and I was allowed to withdraw from Scouts. I think she got the idea I would like Cub Scouts because my friend Kurt was in Scouts and was enjoying it. During my frustrating knot-tying efforts I remember James Walker being very encouraging, telling me, "You can do it. Keep trying," but I never successfully learned any knots. I had been sitting on the back steps of the house with my piece of rope, struggling with knots for at least an hour, and it's likely James's mother saw me struggling and told her son to go encourage me. All three of the Walker kids were good kids. I don't remember their father being around, so I imagine Mrs. Walker was probably a widow, renting rooms to increase her income.

In Dhahran there had been no TV, but the Walker family had a TV, a big Motorola console (with built-in record player) that dominated the north end of the living room. But even to nine-year-old me the TV shows on the air after school were ridiculous and boring. *Howdy Doody* was the worst, *The Mickey Mouse Club* second worst. The shows after dinner were just as bad: *I've Got a Secret*, *The Jack Benny Show*, *December Bride*, and other pap too boring to remember.

BUT, there was one after-school TV show that all us kids looked forward to with feverish anticipation. At four o'clock all five of us would stop what we were doing and take our accustomed places in the living room in front of the TV because *Commander 9* was coming on the air.

Commander 9 was a locally produced show on KMBC Channel 9. It was thirty minutes long and featured a station employee in a half-baked space uniform seated in front of a plywood and cardboard control panel with a big TV screen above it. He would introduce the show, which consisted of episodes of *Flash Gordon* serial movies from the 1930s. After some suitably ominous and dramatic words from Commander 9, the camera would move up to the "control screen," which would show a spiral pattern of black and white stripes spinning hypnotically. This was accompanied by a frisson of futuristic electronic music.

We eyed the hypnotic spinning disc with a mix of fascination and delicious fear. Tommy would shout, "Don't look at it, you'll be hypnotized and go crazy!" Pandemonium usually ensued as we wriggled in fright and anticipation, racing around the living room trying to stay out of range of the hypnotic screen. Tommy usually ducked behind the couch; Alice and my sister usually ran from the room. I braced myself, gritted my teeth, and squinted at the disc, hoping for the best. James, older and wiser, calmly advised holding our breaths to counteract the hypnosis. Then, after a commercial, we would be catapulted into another *Flash Gordon* episode.

Each day the episode would end with Flash in perilous danger, sometimes threatened by the hawk men, sometimes by a tyrannosaurus with Maine lobster claws, sometimes by Ming's ape-men. Charles Middleton played Ming the Merciless, dressed in a high-collared robe and skullcap. Despite the awful strait Flash found himself in, we knew that he would fight his way out of it in the next episode. Sometimes story continuity was ignored, and Flash would appear in an entirely different scene the next day, but no matter, it was action that counted. And there was plenty of that, along with exotic creatures, strange alien people, and the alluring Princess Aura (I liked her, with her sultry evil scheming, better than blonde and helpless Dale Arden). The show had lots of adventure, bravery, and an underlying optimism.

When the show ended, the five of us would immediately begin reenacting that episode, which would then merge with previous episodes. Each of us chose a part, and sometimes several of us would be playing the same character: Flash or Prince Barin or Dale Arden, or Queen Azura or Ming himself. We'd often slip effortlessly from one character to another as the fast-evolving plot required. We embellished the plot as we went along, repeating key scenes in infinite variation, racing around the living room until Mrs. Walker would step out of the kitchen where she had been drinking coffee with my mother and tell us to quit racketing around, ". . . so loud I can't hear myself think."

As I look back on those hours of great fun and high excitement I realize we were also internalizing the positive values Flash and his colleagues exemplified: bravery in the cause of right, support of friends and allies, truthfulness, honor. And since we needed all the actors we could get, all five of us were included every time. No exclusion of the girls because they were girls, or Tommy because he was too little. We never hurt each other either physically or with criticism.

We came to understand that, like Flash, if we were optimistic, worked hard, helped our friends, fought against injustice, and always tried to do the right thing, everything would come out all right. That no matter how bad things looked today, tomorrow would be better.

Pretty good life lessons. Thanks, Flash.

Cold weather came to Kansas City, and one day there was a dusting of snow. Beautiful! I enjoyed scuffing through the snow on my way to and from school. At school we couldn't go outside at recess but instead stayed inside and played basketball in the school gym.

Christmas vacation came. Mrs. Walker and the Walker kids left for a week to visit relatives. One evening a heavy snow started right after dinner. After I went up to bed, I slid the curtains on the window near the head of my bed open a bit and watched the snow drifting silently down past the yellow glow of the streetlight on Virginia Avenue. It was silent except for the soft sound of the furnace. The snow, the silent house—it all seemed both cozy and melancholy.

My mother told us we'd be driving to Grandmother Grace's farm for Christmas Eve and Christmas Day, then back to Kansas City. "We'll take all our presents with us and open them at Grandma's. But we can't leave Mrs. Walker's house untended for very long, so we'll drive back here the afternoon of Christmas Day."

December 24 was overcast with a sharpness in the air that I had learned meant more snow was coming. We loaded up the car and drove to Grandmother Juna's house. My sister and I sat on the couch, bored, while my aunt Bonnie and Grandmother Juna described their Christmas activities to my mother in endless detail.

It was almost three o'clock by the time we said our goodbyes, went carefully down the slippery front steps to the car, and started off.

The streets weren't too snow-covered. Out of town, Highway 29 north to Atchison had patches of snow that traffic had turned to ice. My mother was driving slowly and carefully. It was getting dark by the time we crossed the big steel trestle bridge over the Missouri River and drove through the town of Atchison, Kansas.

Cars had their headlights on in the hazy dusk. By the time we got out of Atchison and onto two-lane Route 114, it was dark and light snow was blowing across the beam of our headlights.

My mother had the wheel in a firm grip with both hands and was leaning forward in the seat. I could tell she was nervous. The snow and wind had increased. There were no other cars in sight on the narrow two-lane blacktop. It was getting hard to see the road in the accumulating snow since this part of Kansas is board-flat. Worse, the old blacktop road made a number of sharp ninety-degree turns to skirt around people's farms.

We were just creeping along. "There's a road sign," I told my mother as I sighted the Kansas Route 17 sign. We kept slowly moving ahead in the blizzard. We only had glimpses of the edge of the asphalt to know where the road was. Suddenly there was no road. My mother put the brakes on, but the tires slid slid and the car eased gently into the shallow ditch alongside the road. She tried reverse, but the tires spun; she tried going forward again but the tires just spun. We were stuck.

She turned off the engine and lights. "Both of you put your boots and coats on."

I did so while my mother helped my sister into her boots.

I peered into the darkness. The snowstorm abated for a moment and I saw a light. "There's a light over there," I said. I could see a house with a yellow yard light not more than fifty yards ahead.

"We'll walk there and get help," my mother said. We stepped out into the snow and wind and began trudging toward the light.

I rather enjoyed walking through the snowstorm. As we walked we could identify where the road was by feel, under the accumulating snow. The house was a typical Kansas farmhouse—square, one story, and non-descript. As we approached, an older woman opened the door. "Saw you coming. Come inside quick, the wind's a-blowin' tonight." A man was sitting in a rocking chair reading a newspaper. The old woman ushered us over to the woodstove. "These folks have got car trouble, Ed."

"Not surprised on a night like this. Where you tryin' to get to?"

"Effingham," my mother told him. "Grace Trial is my mother-in-law. We're going to spend Christmas with her."

He nodded. "The widow Grace. Talbert family. From up near Muscotah."

"Yes."

We all stood in silence around the cheery woodstove, which was keeping the one-room combination kitchen, dining room, and sitting room quite comfortable. The place had a certain smell, not unpleasant. I could see that this old couple spent most of their time in this single room. There were tools in one corner, work clothes hung on a row of pegs, no pictures, no books, and the windows were covered for the winter with tacked-up vinyl.

"Well," the man said, laying his *Atchison Globe* newspaper aside. "Ya'll wait here. It takes a little time to get the tractor started when it's cold."

"Oh I hate to see you go to all this trouble," my mother said. But we all knew there wasn't any alternative.

He went into the tiny coatroom where he donned tall black rubber boots, a muffler, a plaid hat with earflaps, and a worn and stained coat. He grabbed a big flashlight and disappeared into the blizzard.

An hour later he returned. "Got your car pulled outta the ditch. Wasn't bent up none. I pulled her up here to the house and got her started to warm up."

My mother thanked him effusively.

"You folks better foller me to the widow's house," he told my mother. "Cain't hardly see the road, but I know this area real good. You just drive real slow behind the tractor. No lights on the old tractor but I know these roads. I got the log chain in case you get stuck again."

"Goodbye and thank you again," my mother told the old lady. "I'm very, very grateful for your help tonight. . . ."

"Ain't nothin'. Folks always help each other around here. Merry Christmas."

We drove at a walking pace fifteen feet behind the old tractor in the blowing snow, keeping it in our headlights. In a few minutes we were at Grandmother's house.

The old man turned the tractor around and disappeared into the blizzard with a wave, still driving with no lights, sitting unprotected on the bare tractor seat in the blowing snow.

As we all warmed up by Grandmother's coal stove, Mother told her the story.

"Ed and Betty Ames," Grandmother Grace said. "Good folks."

Good folks indeed.

Spring 1955 came, and soon it was the last day of school, then glorious summer vacation.

On clear breezy days James and I would walk over to the parkway between the lanes on Paseo Boulevard and just wander around or play catch with a soft rubber ball he had. The parkway was a hundred-foot-wide neatly landscaped area between the north- and southbound lanes. It ran for ten or twelve long blocks, and sometimes James and I would walk the entire length of it. At several points there were decorative amphitheater-like curved steps four or five steps high and a pergola at the top. We would pretend these were temples and palaces of ancient Rome. We could enact stories of Roman Centurions and invading Vandals.

"Why are you stopping?" James asked, as I stood silent in the shade of the pergola.

"Just thinking."

"About what?"

"When I was six years old I went with my parents to see Roman ruins in Lebanon and at a desert town in Syria called Palmyra."

"I never heard of those places."

We sat down in the shade in a companionable silence.

I daydreamed about ancient Palmyra. It had been winter when we visited, and the desert wind was cold. We had spent the night in a comfortable government-operated hotel at the ruins. It was the off-season, so we were the only guests. The next morning we meandered around the ruined temples and stone roadway. I clambered up on some of the big blocks of stone while my father took pictures. Behind me the valley of tombs was absolutely silent in the cold morning light. I asked my father how long those monuments had stood there in this desert.

"About twelve hundred years. Queen Zenobia ruled ancient Palmyra when it was a powerful trade city on the caravan route between the Arabian Gulf and Damascus. But Palmyra was conquered by the Roman Army, and after a period of time the city declined. It's been ruins for over a thousand years."

But today it was a summer day in Kansas City. I touched one of the stone (actually concrete) columns of the graceful pergola that formed a semi-circle in the park. "Someday this will be ruins too," I intoned portentously, imagining myself to be a Roman Tribune surveying a conquered city.

We sat for a while then started walking up the wide grassy parkway toward the next little park. Ruins were in the past; today we were alive and had a sunny day to explore. We kept walking northward until about 20th Street; then we were tired, so we walked over to Troost and caught the southbound streetcar back to the 44th Street stop. For our rides home, my mother and Mrs. Walker had given James and me streetcar tokens, which reminded me of ancient coins we had bought from vendors at the ruins of Baalbek and Palmyra. The coins were probably counterfeits made for tourists like us, but no matter, they were magical, calling up the ghosts of ancient civilizations.

When James and I got home we found Tommy in the backyard. My sister and Alice were in the house somewhere.

"Where'd you go?" Tommy asked James.

"Nowhere," James told him. The three of us trooped into the kitchen where Mrs. Walker let us each have a glass of cherry Kool-Aid. We no longer played at *Flash Gordon* since it was no longer on TV. At the end of the school term the TV station had wisely assumed that *Commander 9*'s school-kid audience was unlikely to be inside the house at four in the afternoon, so without fanfare *Commander 9* went off the air.

In mid-summer I spent a week at Grandmother Grace's farm.

She welcomed my company at her farm at the edge of the village of Effingham, Kansas. She grazed four Guernsey cows on half the acreage and had a man come in and bale hay on the other half. The hay bales were stored in a loft in the old barn and used to feed the cows through the winter. She had a large garden with beans, potatoes, corn, cucumbers (which she made into really great pickles), and sometimes strawberries. There were about twenty chickens in a coop with an open area for them to walk around in during the day. At night she'd close up the coop with them inside "To keep varmints out." She milked the four Guernsey cows by hand every morning, kept the cream and milk she needed, and sold the rest to a man who came around in his ramshackle truck to pick up the milk can. She canned vegetables every summer and stored potatoes in a low-ceilinged root cellar under the house. The root cellar was kind of a neat place. It was also the storm cellar, where you could take shelter when a tornado threatened. One never did while I was visiting. The entrance to the cellar was outside the house. You'd go out the back door and beside the little porch were two wooden doors set at an angle to get into the cellar. Open one of the doors, go down four or five uneven concrete steps, and you'd be in the dirt-walled room with a single light bulb with a pull cord. It was only five feet high and eight feet square, with rough-cut wooden shelves where the canned goods in jars and the potatoes in boxes were kept.

Her house was about seven hundred square feet, wood frame, set on short pillars of stone mortared together to provide a crawl space underneath. But I didn't crawl in there, having been warned that there were spiders under there (which there were). Inside the house was a combined dining room and kitchen where she spent almost all her time, and there was a tiny sitting room, a bedroom, and an indoor bathroom that had been added a few years before when she'd gotten rid of the outhouse.

She never spent any time in the sitting room, which had a bookcase, two dusty armchairs with doilies on the backs, a tiny round table with a lamp on it, and a window with lace curtains. I liked that room. There was a handmade throw rug on the floor, and I would sit on it leafing through *National Geographic* and *Life* magazines, many of them dating back to the 1940s. There were also a half dozen scrapbooks with newspaper articles from WWII-era newspapers that she had assembled when her son, my father, was in the army. I found them fascinating—the articles, the ads, and the many advertisements to buy war bonds, or to volunteer for the Red Cross, or to donate scrap metal.

The door to the adjoining bedroom was a standard door, but the door to the dining room was a double sliding door with glass panels. The woodstove in the dining room was the only source of heat, so during the winter the sitting room door was kept closed and the bedroom door open.

Summer mornings were silent—the grass and the shrubbery drenched with dew in the deep green and gold morning light. I spent many hours roaming her farm. There were few trees, this being prairie land, but it was fun feeling the dry heat of a summer sun, listening to the insects chirring, feeling the dry grass of the pasture. I kept my distance from the cows placidly grazing in the pasture or lying in the shade.

The best feature of the farm was the old barn. On the ground floor were the milking stalls for the cows, each with an oak stanchion that would hold their head in place so they wouldn't move around while my grandmother milked them. I liked to run my hand over the edges of the stanchions, which had been worn smooth by decades of cows. There was a ladder built on to the wall of the barn that led to the dusty hayloft. Upstairs with the fragrant hay bales, light beams coming through splits in the wooden walls, it was cool and silent. Dusty cobwebs billowed slowly in the hay-scented air. Summer heat lay outside, but inside it was comfortably cool and dark with mystery. I loved that old barn with its mysterious hayloft.

Soon after I arrived back in Kansas City, Mrs. Walker and my mother announced they were taking all five of us kids down to the Palace Movie Theater on the Plaza for the matinee showing of a movie called *20,000 Leagues Under the Sea*. I knew Jules Verne had written a book by that name, and I may even have looked at it on a library shelf once, but it seemed very dry, so I had not tried to read it. Little did I know what a transformative experience that movie would be. We piled into Mrs. Walker's station wagon for the short drive to the theater.

The Palace Theater was, as its name implied, a vast and glorious 1940s theater with chandeliers, two levels of balconies, and red plush seats (a bit worn and stained, but still impressive). The theater staff wore uniforms of short-waisted red jackets and little round black hats. We filed in quietly, overawed by the grandeur all around us.

In a front-row balcony seat we sat in a row twitching with anticipation. Soon the house lights dimmed, the screen lit, and the curtain (yes, there was a real curtain across the screen) drew back. The Buena Vista logo dissolved into rippling blue, a book appeared, coming toward the screen, and opened to reveal the title page of the book: *Twenty Thousand Leagues Under the Sea*. The page turned and we saw the first paragraph of the first chapter "strange rumors of a sea monster in 1868 . . ." First there was some boring scene-setting in San Francisco with Professor Aronnax, Peter Lorre as Conseil, and a ridiculously overplayed Ned Land (Kirk Douglas). But despite this we were enthralled, gaping in wide-eyed silence at the bilious VistaVision color. After we endured Kirk Douglas's singing and playing straight man to a cute seal, the story finally got going. The mysterious sea monster rams the ship our heroes are on, and Aronnax, Conseil, and Land are adrift in a foggy ocean. Then . . . the hooked beak of the *Nautilus* submarine appears in the mist. We were absolutely thrilled with the ominous mystery of this fantastic machine, all iron plates and rivets.

Our heroes clamber aboard the iron monster and creep inside, where they find a Victorian wonderland—clockwork brass instruments, oil paintings, plush red velvet settee, and a pipe organ. The ship is eerily empty of people. Through the forward viewing port they see a party of men in fantastical diving gear conducting a funeral ceremony, then they return to the ship, coming up through an ingenious water port in the bottom.

Then . . . Captain Nemo appears! The dark and mysterious James Mason delivered a masterful performance as the dark and mysterious Captain Nemo. We thrashed and twitched with excitement and fearful pleasure as the story unfolded. The Victorian luxury of his private submarine, his private island, the nuclear engines of the sub, the wonders of the sea, Captain Nemo's dark past, his vendetta against arms dealers and slave traders, his turgid playing of Bach on a Victorian pipe organ, Cannibal Island, and the climactic squid fight. We cowered back in our seats as squid tentacles reached into the *Nautilus*.

And then, the *Nautilus* sinks with a prophetic voice-over by Mason. We were paralyzed with awe, our imaginations on fire. My mother and Mrs. Walker paraded us out into a hot Kansas City afternoon that now seemed monochrome. We were stunned and bleary-eyed as we piled into the station wagon, but we came alive as we drove down Troost Avenue. We began furtively acting out certain snippets of the scenes, becoming more and more absorbed in our roles, slithering and shoving in the crowded back seat until my mother turned and told us, "You're making such a rumpus back there Mrs. Walker can't drive. Be quiet!"

We contained ourselves for a moment then continued sotto voce with furtive glances and small twitching movements until at last we pulled into the driveway. Then the five of us tumbled out onto the lawn shouting orders, posturing, harpooning, battling squids and cannibals and sharks, growling threats against the merchants of death, firing cannon blasts at the gun powder island.

James had a headlock on Tommy as they tumbled onto the lawn. From that first enactment, James owned the role of the giant squid. The rest of us swarmed over him, wrestling, thrashing, and harpooning.

James had Tommy's head pinched in a leg lock and my head pinioned under his arm, Alice and Lindy danced and screamed with pleasure as this tangle of arms and legs rolled down the sloping lawn to the sidewalk. James began to embellish his role by adding "squid sounds," which were a strange combination of moaning and hissing.

Then Tommy and I broke free and the scene changed to Cannibal Island as we raced into the house, through the living room, slowing to a walk as we passed through the kitchen where Mrs. Walker and my mother were drinking coffee, then bursting out the back screen door and sprinting around the house to the front yard where two or three Ned Lands led the race to the beach, the cannibals close behind. We paddled frantically for the safety of the *Nautilus* (the living room), where we piled out of the imaginary row boat and donned diving gear and slipped underwater to grab the treasure on a sunken galleon. Then someone called for us to be back at the island, and we scattered to avoid cannibal spears. Kids raced over chair backs and under tables like deer running from a forest fire. The noise level reached new heights. Mrs. Walker stood in the kitchen doorway eyeing the pandemonium until three Captain Nemos and one Ned Land hunkered down in silence. "With this racket I can't hear myself think!" she announced. We squatted, attempting to look contrite as she continued to eye us, doubtless formulating some suitable punishment. The room was silent. Then from behind the couch came a horrible moaning and hissing, followed by mysterious crawling and thumping sounds. An arm and one leg heaved into view and soon the giant squid, in the form of James, pulled itself around the end of the couch, giant sucker-lined arms flailing and grasping for victims. It was James's finest performance. Until he saw his mother standing stony-faced. He froze, then with a certain dignity pulled himself back to cower behind the couch.

Mrs. Walker muttered, "You kids and your tomfoolery!" and returned to the kitchen. It didn't occur to me until years later to wonder how quiet it would need to be to hear yourself think. No matter. Mrs. Walker was the law, and she ruled with fairness and a degree of latitude, but there was no doubt in our minds that when she said something, we would have to do as she said.

We got to our feet, James emerged from behind the couch, and we filed silently out the front door and onto the lawn.

In late summer my father returned to Kansas City for a couple of weeks. I remember being glad to see him, but his presence didn't change my routine of wandering the nearby streets, or roaming the park on Paseo with James, or sometimes walking to Troost School to swing on the swings. My mother and father's quiet joy at being back together again made us kids feel happy.

One morning after breakfast with Mrs. Walker (she insisted on cooking a big breakfast for all of us every day), my father announced to her that we'd be gone for a couple of days. "First to visit my mother in Kansas, then we're going drive around Missouri a bit and visit Columbia, where we both went to the university."

"The kids can stay with me," Mrs. Walker volunteered, but my mother said she wanted all four of us to spend the time together. "We'll be back by Wednesday or Thursday at the latest."

We packed our luggage into Bonnie's car and drove north to Atchison, then west to Effingham. "We're just going to stop for lunch at Grandma's house, then get on the road to Nevada, Missouri," my father told us.

It was a bright morning and the drive to Effingham was uneventful. My father drove slowly down Main Street and back, which was only three blocks long. He was shaking his head. "Things have really changed in the last few years. The town is dying."

On Main Street the old wooden buildings were vacant and sagging, except for old Mr. Haas's dry goods store. There was a modern gas station at the edge of town. My father turned the car down one of the gravel side streets. The church was closed up. A few houses still had neat flowerbeds and well-tended gardens, but most houses were abandoned. Most of the nearby farms had been bought by corporations that farmed thousands of acres at a time. Farm kids had long since departed for Topeka or Kansas City, never to return.

At my grandmother Grace's house we had a nice fried chicken lunch with gooseberry pie for dessert. I ate two slices. Then while the adults talked I took my little sister on a tour of the farm (I considered myself an expert on this farm ever since my visit earlier in the summer). The last stop was my favorite place, the hayloft in the old barn. But she didn't like the dusty darkness so we went down the ladder and back to the house.

Soon I heard my father calling, and we all piled in the car and set off down the road again. "I think this is where I ran off the road last Christmas," my mother said, pointing down the asphalt to a weather-beaten farmhouse. It all seemed very pleasant now—the flat asphalt road with its right-angle turns, the sun on the hayfields and cattle pastures—but it had been scary that snowy night. After a minute my mother put away the map she had been studying. "Instead of the same old route, let's try a new route. How about this: south on Kansas Highway 59, then cross into Missouri, and south to Nevada on Highway 71." My father smiled at her. "Sure, we have plenty of time."

The flat Kansas farmland did not vary mile after mile. I daydreamed as the car rolled down the endless straight asphalt and the hot summer wind blew in the open windows. I daydreamed of another car trip, a different hot wind blowing in the windows of a car. We had stopped for a few days in Ceylon last year on our way from Dhahran to Kansas City. My father had hired a car to drive us up into the highlands where we could spend the night in the city of Kandy. We'd first driven the long plains of coastal Ceylon, then started up into the foothills of the central highlands. The air got slowly cooler and the land around us greener as we drove. It had been late afternoon when we arrived, and after tea on the terrace of the Queen's Hotel, we had the driver take us to the botanical gardens, where we wandered the paths through the tropical plants as the sun set. A foggy mist had settled over the park by the time we left. I daydreamed of dinosaurs roaming through the mist and ferns. The next day we drove to an elephant farm, where I was given an elephant ride, then we drove back down to the Galle Face Hotel in Colombo. As we left the green highlands on the winding road down to the plain, the air became warm, then hot, just like the Kansas wind coming in the car window now—hot and dry and scented with hayfield stubble.

A signpost announced the town of Oskaloosa.

"An Indian name," my father told us. "The Pottawatomie tribe . . ."

I laughed. "That's a funny name."

"Yes it does sound funny," he said. "Our words probably sounded funny to them too."

I asked why all the road signs had a big yellow flower on them.

"It's a sunflower. The Kansas state flower," my mother told us.

"What's Missouri's state flower?" Linden asked.

"I don't remember," Mother said. "I'll have to look it up when we get home."

There were four pickup trucks parked in the gas station at the edge of town. Four farmers, all dressed alike in faded bib overalls and straw hats, were leaning against one truck talking. They eyed us as we drove slowly past. Most of the stores on Main Street were boarded up just like Effingham. The row of wooden-fronted stores looked like the set of a Western movie except for the concrete sidewalk.

My mother said, "Let's stop and take a look in that old store. Just for fun. We have plenty of time."

The rusty steel sign nailed above the door said *Schotte Dry Goods*. We trooped in through a creaking screen door. It was silent and cool inside. Two ceiling fans coated with dust turned slowly. The ceiling was made of patterned plates of sheet metal painted white.

In the air of the store was a scent compounded of hand tools, gloves, overalls, bags of seed, bags of pelletized fertilizer, and other nameless things. I wandered down a dim and crowded aisle, breathing in the aroma, brushing my hands along folded OshKosh overalls, bags of seed corn, strange devices for doctoring cattle and pigs. Along the back wall of the store was a row of shovels, pickaxes, axes, pitchforks, galvanized washtubs, and other implements whose use I could not guess. The store felt like Aladdin's cave, a treasure trove not of jewels but of mysterious devices only useful to farm folk. I wandered back to the front of the store, where my mother was purchasing a dress for my sister. "Two forty-nine," the old man said, clunking the keys on a huge mechanical cash register. The little white cards stood up, announcing $2.49. He punched two more keys. "Two fifty-nine with tax."

He didn't smile, just stood there in his faded overalls, waiting.

He seemed to me like the fields and the garden and the barn at my grandmother's farm, content to live a silent life, conditioned by sun and shade, cold and heat.

My father was tapping his fingers on the steering wheel as we climbed in. The sun was blinding after the cathedral-like dimness of the store.

"This is a nice dress," my mother told my sister as we drove south. She smiled. "Let's call this your Oskaloosa dress."

In a photo of school kids on the front porch of Valley Springs School on the last day of school in May 1957, my sister is wearing that dress.

We stopped for dinner at a restaurant on the square in Nevada, Missouri (fried chicken with green beans and mashed potatoes, as usual), then drove to a motel to spend the night. I was eyeing the little swimming pool, but Mother said, "It's too late to go swimming."

The next morning we ate a big breakfast at a cafe on the square (fried eggs, bacon, and toast with homemade strawberry jam, as usual). I had put my swimming suit on under my jeans, hoping I could take a swim before we left the motel. But no such luck.

In the car, my mother pointed as she told told my sister and me, "I grew up in that house—205 Central Avenue." We drove by a two-story house with four tall columns on the front porch. I tried to look interested, but I'd much rather have been swimming in the motel pool. It was only nine o'clock in the morning but already hot and humid. No air-conditioning in the car, of course. We then drove by the tiny campus of Cottey College. "That's where your aunt Bonnie went to college," Mother told us. "She was on the yearbook committee. She was good at academics and very popular." My mother sighed and sat staring straight ahead as we drove out of the town of Nevada then east on Highway 60.

My mother was probably wondering why her older sister Bonnie, who had good looks and was outgoing, smart, and ambitious, had never married and had spent her whole adult life in Kansas City, while Mother herself had travelled the world.

I wonder that myself.

It was mid-afternoon by the time we reached the tiny town of Cabool. My father explained to my sister and me that there was a farm here he was considering buying as a retirement home.

We drove down a succession of gravel roads and eventually found the right farm. The realtor and the owners and my parents talked interminably in the sweltering living room while my sister and I fidgeted. I was hoping we would get going soon so we'd get to the next motel so I could go swimming. I told this to my father. The realtor flashed a toothy grin and waved expansively at the fields and woods in front of the house. "Another nice feature of this property is the swimming hole. There's a nice little creek that flows through the property within walking distance of the house. Why don't we all walk down there and you, young man, can take a dip in the swimming hole."

The swimming hole turned out to be a pleasant willow-shaded spot on a tiny creek just down the hill from the house. I slipped off my shoes, jeans, and tee shirt and waded in while my mother and sister sat at the creek's edge, shoes off, their feet in the water.

The creek was only four feet deep, but had a nice pebbled bottom, so it was fun ducking under the water and examining the colored stones. I saw a few tiny fish and some crayfish among the stones.

Walking back to the house through some tall weeds, a grasshopper flew up from the grass and landed on my sister's bare arm. She let out a shriek that scared us all. My mother rushed to her and brushed the grasshopper off and consoled Lindy, who insisted on being carried the rest of the way to the car, sobbing the whole time. We said our goodbyes and drove away.

We spent the night at a roadside motel north of Cabool (with no swimming pool). The next morning we drove north on Highway 63 to Columbia, where we ate lunch at Glenn's Cafe. Then a driving tour past the university campus while my parents pointed out various things to each other. "There's the boarding house at 301 Conley," my mother said. "It looks the same."

"The same as when you were here as a student or when we were here after the war?"

She chuckled, "Both I guess. Some things will never change." She glanced at her watch. "Almost time to go meet the Dawsons." My father drove out Highway 40, then south a half mile on State Road UU.

"Double horseshoe lane," my sister remarked on seeing the road sign. "So it is," my mother said.

We turned into a gravel driveway at a mailbox stenciled *J. Dawson RFD 3*. While my parents talked to the Dawsons, Linden and I and the two Dawson girls sat in silence. Eva was round faced and cheerfully silent. Her older sister, Marion, said little but giggled often at what we heard the adults talking about at the kitchen table. A smile broke over her face she heard her grandfather describing the hogs as 'ornery'. I laughed too, mostly at her big smile, not quite sure what ornery meant.

Soon we piled back into the car and set out for Kansas City on Highway 40. My parents talked about the Dawson farm while my sister and I dozed in the back seat.

I didn't realize it until much later, but during that afternoon my parents decided to buy the Dawson farm. That decision changed all our lives. My parents could have retired to Modesto or any other town in California like most of my father's colleagues, who were originally from California. But my mother wanted to live in Missouri, on a farm. And so my childhood and my sister's became tied to Missouri. I am now retired and am living on the farm my parents decided to buy on that sunny afternoon in 1955. And I like it.

A day or two after we returned to Kansas City, my father told my sister and me he was leaving to return to Dhahran and work. He said he would be back in a few months. The next day all of us rode with him in a taxi to Union Station to see him off on a train to New York. It wasn't an emotional event. Mother was calm and we were quite sure the four of us would be together again soon.

I wasn't aware of it at the time, but my father had been offered the position of director of the TAPline Training Center in Sidon, Lebanon. He and my mother had decided he should take the job. Both my mother and father wanted the family to be back together again. At first Mother was reluctant, but she had talked it over with her sister Bonnie, who convinced her she should go with him. "Mother is better now. Your time here has cheered her up," Bonnie told her. "And I plan to retire at the end of this school year, so I'll soon have plenty of free time to care for Mother."

When my father got back to Dhahran, he prepared to leave for Sidon. There was still a good bit of household goods at his house in Dhahran, left there when we'd moved to Kansas City. The company arranged to ship his household goods to Sidon, but he couldn't take everything.

His diary entry for moving day says: "All bags and boxes packed very full . . . I had to leave behind the box of wooden blocks worn smooth by small hands." My father seldom showed much emotion, but at heart he was a rather sentimental man. The toy blocks he was writing about were the blocks I had played with on the floor of the house in Dhahran. It was only after my father died and I was reading his diaries that I remembered those blocks. They were simple sanded but unpainted bits of two by four, needing only imagination to become vehicles, buildings, mountains, even people and animals. My sister and I spent many happy hours playing with those blocks.

On September 27, 1955, my father moved into his dorm room at the training center in Sidon, Lebanon.

My father's diary entries during this period are full of enthusiasm—he likes his new assignment, he likes Lebanon, he likes his co-workers. The Sidon Training Center is a small complex of new buildings located on the coast adjacent to the oil storage tanks and tanker loading facility, which was the Mediterranean end of TAPline, the Trans-Arabia Pipeline. The Sidon Training Center (STC) was set up to provide an orientation course for new American employees coming to Saudi Arabia and to coordinate advanced Saudi Arab training at the American University of Beirut. Lebanon's climate and topography are much like southern California, with temperate weather and rain on the Mediterranean side of the coastal mountain range, and desert on the inland side.

Back in Missouri I prepared for the start of school, but before classes started my mother took my sister and me on a drive to Lawrence, Kansas, for reasons I don't remember. We spent the night in a motel in Lawrence, and it happened to be my birthday. My mother presented me with a book called *All About Dinosaurs* by Roy Chapman Andrews, who was something of a famous personage in fossil studies in those days. It was great! All kids like dinosaurs, and I was no exception.

A month later, on a crisp and clear autumn Saturday, my mother took my sister and me downtown on the streetcar to get our vaccinations for our trip to Lebanon. We each got injected multiple times—for typhoid, typhus, diphtheria, etc. This was a ritual associated with overseas travel in those days, and we accepted it. When we emerged from the doctor's office the day had turned hot. By the time we'd walked to the streetcar stop, my arm was aching and my stomach was queasy. Riding the overheated streetcar was a nauseating experience.

In early September 1955 I started fourth grade at Troost School. Kurt was no longer a classmate since his parents had moved to Prairie Village, Kansas, a comfortable suburb on the west side of Kansas City. One Saturday we drove out to visit them. Kurt's parents had gotten him involved in scouting, and I remember he had a painting in his room of him on a Scout camping trip. In the painting he was about eight years old, sitting on a log by the campfire, his parents and sister also near the fire. An Indian girl had crept out of the forest behind them and was curiously studying the faces reflected in the fire. Kurt said he liked camping and Scouts. But neither camping nor Cub Scouts ever had much appeal for me.

I soon got to know a new kid in my classroom named Tommy. We talked about airplanes and space ships at recess. I remember walking to his house after school one day. His parents had remodeled the house in sleek 1950s modern. On one wall of the living room was a panel that would slide up, controlled by a wall switch. Behind the panel was a TV set with a seventeen-inch diagonal screen (which was the biggest TV you could buy in those days). Neither Tommy nor I had much interest in watching anything on TV, but both of us liked the sliding panel.

That fall as I began fourth grade at Troost School, I noticed my mother's attitude was different.

I was never very perceptive of my parents' moods so hadn't really noticed that my mother seemed increasingly worn the previous year as her efforts to care for her mother, and the strain of raising kids without her husband, had taken their toll. But I did notice now that she seemed much happier. I realize now that this was because two decisions had been made: to buy the farm in Columbia, and for us all to be together again in Lebanon.

Thanksgiving came and went. My mother was a member of the Troost School PTA and helped our third-grade teacher arrange a small Christmas party the last day of school before the Christmas holidays.

I remember nothing about the party, but I found my mother had kept the thank-you notes Kurt and I had written to her (at the teacher's direction, I am sure).

The next weekend my mother drove out to Prairie Village to say goodbye to Kurt's parents. This is when I first learned that we would be moving from Kansas City to Sidon, Lebanon. I awkwardly said goodbye to Kurt, but neither one of us felt particularly saddened—kids are resilient. Back at our rental house I overheard my mother talking to Mrs. Walker. "We're going to move overseas next month. My sister Bonnie has decided to retire next June, so she'll be able to care for Mother. So . . ."

"I'm sorry to see you go," Mrs. Walker told her. "You've been the best tenants I've ever had. And the kids get along so well . . . but I'm happy you'll be together as a family over there."

I have no memory of saying goodbye to the Walker kids. They had seemed like siblings to me, but now that had ended. The memory of that sad farewell has been erased by the years. I never saw James and Tommy and Alice again. But I had moved before, leaving friends behind. And I knew that we would probably move again. I accepted the fact I would leave friends behind, and that I would make new friends at my new home.

I looked around at my room for one last time, went down the stairs, and got in the car.

We stayed temporarily at Grandmother Juna's house on Garfield Avenue while my mother sorted our things—some to be put in storage and some to be shipped to Sidon. After a couple of nights at Grandmother's house, my mother moved us to the Berkshire Hotel at 1021 East Linwood Boulevard.

I recently found the receipt for our stay at the Berkshire Hotel: room 215, $32.64. Why would my mother and father have kept it for all these years?

Her decision to stay in a hotel was a good one. We still went to Grandmother's house every day, but it was good to leave the small cluttered house on Garfield Avenue after dinner.

Mother's sadness over leaving Mrs. Walker and her kids lifted quickly, as did any lingering doubts she may have had about leaving her mother and sister behind. She laughed a lot as she told her mother and sister at the dinner table about the Christmas vacation in Switzerland that she and my father had decided on. We'd fly to Rome for a few days, then to Milan for a few days, then enjoy Christmas in Zermatt, Switzerland.

My mother talked about a visit to Rome in 1948 when my aunt Bonnie had joined my mother and father and me for a few days.

"Remember how cold and windy it was?"

Bonnie laughed, "But you insisted we take an open carriage ride around the Colosseum. I was freezing."

"I'm glad you met us in San Francisco last summer," my mother told Aunt Bonnie. "I'll never forget the sight of you meeting us as the ship docked, waving a hatchet you had bought for Mike." They both laughed and I suddenly remembered that hatchet with its leather sheath—must have been put in storage.

"I'll miss you and Mother," I heard my mother say. "But . . ."

"You need to be with your husband," Aunt Bonnie stated positively. "I'll be fine here and so will Mother. My retirement is only seven months away."

We left the Berkshire Hotel early on the morning of December 10 in a taxi to Union Station, where we boarded the Missouri Pacific train for St. Louis. The December Missouri countryside flowed by, dusted with snow, looking very bleak in the pale morning light. In St. Louis we changed trains and were shown to our compartment on the overnight train to New York. It was fun sleeping on the moving train in a fold-down bed with its own little privacy curtain. The next morning we arrived at Grand Central Station, collected our luggage, and took a taxi to the Plaza Hotel. Manhattan was bright with Christmas decorations. After checking into our room, we wandered around the streets enjoying the festive store window displays. The PA system in front of Bergdorf Goodman was playing "Silver Bells," which I really liked. "Just like the stores on the Plaza last Christmas," my sister told my mother. Mother stared at the window display for a long time, her mind clearly elsewhere, and I realized then that for her, leaving familiar Kansas City, her mother, her sister, and the Walkers was not as easy as she had made it look.

The next day we took a taxi to the Museum of Natural History. I enjoyed the dinosaur displays, but then I found the Hayden Planetarium sign advertising a matinee show. I persuaded my mother that we needed to see that show. We had lunch at the cafeteria in the museum, then filed into the planetarium. It was crowded with people in a holiday mood. The lights dimmed, and on the domed ceiling all the stars came out. I was breathless. It was like viewing the night sky on the clearest night possible. The show included descriptions of the planets. Mars and Jupiter were wonderful, and at one point the announcer said they could show the night sky as it would have looked a million years ago. The stars slowly shifted position as the years rolled back hundreds of years per second. It was great! Time travel and space travel. The show included simulation of a supernova, views of colliding galaxies, blue stars and red stars and yellow stars. I was enthralled.

From that afternoon until this day I have been fascinated by space, other planets, other stars, all of the universe around us. I still liked reading about dinosaurs, but now I wanted to read more about space and about the future, about alien planets and starships.

While we were in New York, my father had moved from Dhahran to a room in the dormitory at the Sidon Training Center. A house had been leased for him and his family but was not ready yet. He signed out for a ten-day vacation, the company car drove him to Beirut, and he caught an Alitalia flight to Rome. In Rome he went to the Lebanese embassy and got a work permit for Lebanon, then spent the night in the Hotel Flora.

On December 14, 1955, my mother checked us out of the Plaza Hotel in Manhattan, and with our four suitcases, we took a taxi to Idlewild Airport. There we boarded the ARAMCO DC-6, *Flying Gazelle*, for the five-hour flight to Gander, Newfoundland, where we would refuel before the transatlantic leg of the journey. This was the standard route in those propeller aircraft days.

We were served dinner on the plane over the Atlantic, which I thought was really fun, and the food was good. We each had a little tray with a tiny tablecloth, china plates, knives and forks, entree, vegetable, a tiny slice of bread, and a little cup of fruit compote for dessert. Then the lights were dimmed and we slept as best we could in the echoing interior of the plane. I woke occasionally and admired the moonlit clouds over the Atlantic. Sunrise came and we were served breakfast (which I thought was as good as the dinner—a tray with white cloth, small knives and forks, eggs (no bacon of course), toast, and honey). We landed in Amsterdam at eleven thirty AM on December 15, 1955. A shuttle bus took us to the Grand Hotel Krasnapolsky, one of the most famous hotels in downtown Amsterdam. It was an ornate grey stone pile on Dam Square, with an elegant dining room and a trendy coffee shop on the first floor. The desk staff and Concierge station personnel , fluent in at least four languages, could tell by clothes and demeanor what nationality guest were. They greeted us in flawless English. Uniformed elevator operators manned two elevators. The rooms were quaint, spotlessly clean, and very quiet despite the bustle and traffic on Dam Square.

The Grand Hotel Krasnapolsky was a hotel that ARAMCO contracted with for rooms for employees passing through Amsterdam. I spent many a night there over the course of the next ten years.

We strolled around Amsterdam admiring the tiny canals, the little shops full of Christmas things. We stopped in a cafe for tea. Then we walked for another hour until jet lag was making us very sleepy, so back to the hotel for dinner as soon as the hotel dining room opened. Then to bed.

The next morning after breakfast in the hotel dining room, we put on our coats and strolled around Amsterdam for an hour. My mother was as happy as I'd ever seen her. It was an adventure, going to Lebanon, and the family would be having the adventure together. We took the hotel shuttle bus to the airport and boarded the *Flying Gazelle* at one thirty for the flight to Rome. I had a window seat. The first hour of the flight we were over a solid layer of clouds, but then over the Alps the clouds broke a bit and I got a few glimpses of impressive snow-covered mountain peaks surrounded by clouds.

We arrived at Fiumicino Airport in Rome at five fifteen PM. My father was waiting for us at the gate. I was happy to see him but felt like it was no big deal. Mother was laughing with happiness. "Linden was shy," my father wrote in his diary. She had seen her father only twice in the last fourteen months, but she soon warmed up. We took a taxi to the Hotel Flora, where we settled into rooms 123 and 124, then we had dinner in the dining room. My parents were all smiles. We went to bed early since we had a train to catch early the next morning.

From my earliest memory I have enjoyed travelling overseas—which I consider one of the best gifts my parents ever gave me. Travel was sometimes tiring, occasionally frustrating, but always interesting. Since childhood I have felt the annoyances of long airplane flights, language difficulties, foreign money, not knowing where to go to get a good dinner, and all the other inconveniences are nothing compared to the great value of the journey itself.

We woke before dawn, dressed, and took a taxi to the train station to catch the six forty-five AM train to Milan and on to Switzerland. We had a compartment to ourselves. I dozed for a time, then watched the Italian countryside flashing by. The train was very clean and fast. Passengers could go to the dining car for meals or have them in their compartments, so we had a wonderful breakfast in our compartment.

The conductor warned my father (in very nice English) that we would have very little time between trains at the Milan station. He had alerted the baggage porter to help us get to our connecting train. As we came to a stop in the Milan station, my father handed suitcases out the window of the compartment to a porter who we followed at a run to the platform where we boarded the train north toward Switzerland. My father and mother thanked the porter profusely and tipped him. My father had bought first-class tickets on this train too, so we had a compartment to ourselves. Uniformed men came down the corridor as the train moved north, saluted, and stamped our passports as we crossed into Switzerland. Our next change of trains was at the small town of Brig (pronounced Breeg), Switzerland. We disembarked into a cold and foggy evening. We were the only people on the train platform waiting for the train that would take us east to Zermatt. Above us on all sides the mountains disappeared up into mist. The tunnel mouth was black. I remember my sister, wearing her gray coat and wool hat, glancing fearfully at the tunnel mouth from time to time.

But after a while a light appeared in the tunnel, the train pulled to a stop and a porter showed us to our cabin on the train, and we efficiently moved eastward. The railway went through a series of tunnels. We would enter a tunnel so fast it was as though a light had been turned off, leaving me staring at my reflection in the glass, then out of the tunnel into dark mountains on all sides and the distant lights of a village. There was much snow on the ground.

We arrived at the Zermatt train station at eight PM. The town was a jewel box of glowing lights on sparkling snow. Two horse-drawn sleighs were waiting to take guests to the Zermatterhof Hotel. It was great fun, our legs warm under the blankets, the horse bells jingling as we trotted down the snow-blanketed main street of Zermatt, all the shops and restaurants aglow.

The next morning dawned clear and bright. We wandered down the main street. (This was in the days before Zermatt became an international resort crowded with tourists.) The town was a picturesque Alpine village with wooden-fronted shops and the Matterhorn towering in the distance. In the afternoon we took a horse-drawn sleigh tour of the village and the frozen lake where people were ice skating and sliding handled stones on the ice—a game called curling.

On the nineteenth of December we took the cog train up the mountain to the Riffelhaus Hotel, arriving at three PM. It was great. Wood-paneled walls, a fire crackling in the fireplace, and a big Christmas tree set up in the lobby. For the first two days we were the only guests. My father lost no time in arranging for my sister and me to take skiing lessons. The ski lift and the beginner slopes were right in the front of the hotel.

Our instructor was a man named Odilo Julen. He (and my parents) laboriously got my sister and me into our boots and skis. Then we learned the basics of moving around on skis, of snowplowing down a gentle slope, and of how to get on and off the rope-pull ski lift. But my sister, only five years old, soon got cold so came inside and didn't take any more lessons. I was nine years old and I quickly learned to love skiing. I took a ski lesson each morning—December 21, 22, 23, and again on December 26. Each day I went up to a higher lift station, Rotenboden, then the topmost one: Gornergrat. Each one was slightly more difficult, but great fun. I fell down a few times, but got right back up and kept going. My father was visibly proud of me.

This was the start of a lifetime enjoyment of skiing. Over the course of my life I haven't skied often; sometimes years would pass without a ski trip, but then I'd pick it up again, starting on the beginner slopes, and it would always be just as much fun as I remembered. For me the enjoyment includes the clear cold air, the mountain scenery, and the crisp smell of pine trees as much as the skiing itself. I've skied in New Mexico, Nevada, California, and Colorado. And once in 1984 I returned to Zermatt to sightsee and ski. The hotel was much the same although the name was now Sport Hotel Riffelberg. It was just as much fun as I remembered, though the shops and ski slopes were now crowded with Japanese tourists.

Before my lesson each day I would usually ride the rope-pull ski lift on the beginner slopes a time or two. On my last day of skiing the sun-bronzed young man working the lift played a joke on me. The rope-pull ski lift pulled skiers up the slope, not with chairs, but with simple steel bars you put behind you as they came by. You would be gently pulled up the slope sliding on your skis. To make it easier for skiers to catch a bar coming up behind them, the attendant would put the bar in your hand while you kept your eyes on the slope ahead of you.

As usual I slid carefully up to the take-off point and readied myself to grab the tow bar and slide up the slope. He handed me a bar from behind and I crouched ready to slide forward. Nothing happened. Only after two or three bars had gone by me did I realize he had handed me a tow bar that was not connected to the rope. He was laughing good-naturedly.

I'm laughing now as I remember nine year old me crouching, staring intently ahead, while holding a bar not connected to the towrope. It was funny.

Christmas Eve we had dinner in the hotel dining room. Mother wore a dress and pearls, father a suit and tie. The menu was asparagus with sauce, consommé, filet mignon and la belle de Mai, pommes Parisienne, with omelette flambee au rhum for dessert. The food was delicious and the service was superb. The woman waiting on our table was wearing a frilly black and white dirdl with a fine lace cap on her head. The dining room lights were turned low; the soft light from the candles on the Christmas tree made our faces glow.

Christmas Day my father's diary says, "A sunny, cold day. We spent the entire day inside the hotel opening our Christmas gifts and enjoying them." I remember that one of my gifts was a book about dinosaurs, *First Book of Prehistoric Animals*.

I still have that book, worn and often read, but in quite good condition and full of nostalgia. I have a number of books from my childhood, each worn but well cared for.

We borrowed a deck of cards from the hotel and played rummy, the four of us, helping Linden win sometimes. It was good quiet fun. Other times I would sit and read. Mother and Father might sometimes go downstairs, put their coats on, and stroll around the terrace viewing the spectacular mountain scenery in crystalline air.

It was Hilton's Shangri-La, Mann's Magic Mountain. Time did not exist. The four of us together were content, unknown Sidon ahead, but I felt no apprehension because it was clear that my parents didn't.

That night clouds were low when we went to bed. I woke in the night and looked out the window; snow was falling, and far down the valley the lights of Zermatt village glowed. I remembered that first heavy snow a year before in Kansas City when I had lain in my bed comfy and warm watching the snow drifting past the yellow streetlight. Now I saw snow drifting past the lights of the village.

The day after Christmas I spent my last hours on the ski slopes. There were a lot of people on the slopes; the air was clear, the sun bright, the mountains beautiful. In the afternoon my mother and I took the cog train down to Zermatt village to return the rented skis. While my mother stopped in a shop I watched men playing curling on a frozen lake.

Two days later, on the twenty-seventh of December, we left Zermatt by train for Milan, arriving at 6:10 PM. We took a taxi from the train station to the Grand Hotel Plaza, checked in, walked around outside, and ate dinner at a businessman's restaurant where my father had tortellini. Antonio was our waiter. My father liked the place and the food so well that we ate dinner there every night we were in Milan.

The next day we walked around in cold and cloudy weather. The hotel was near Cathedral Square, so we looked inside the great echoing cathedral with its ceiling hidden in darkness. The blood-red and blue and dark-yellow stained glass windows, rows of candles glowing, the gold-edged red cloth on the altar—the sense of mystery was very strong. With this kind of psychological power, and the threat of eternal hell,

I could see why the church became an empire after the fall of Rome. At the top of the wooden latticework that was the confessionals, I saw a cobweb waving slowly and remembered the hayloft of my grandmother's barn, where dust motes drifted in shafts of light and cobwebs waved softly in silence. Mystical places, deus loci.

After the cathedral we walked down the street window-shopping. My mother and Linden went into a shop called Borsolino and soon emerged wearing stylish Italian hats.

"You two look great!" my father said. "Very stylish."

I thought the hats looked silly, but was smart enough to keep my opinion to myself.

I loved the Italian paper money. Each denomination was a different size and a different color. A 10,000-lira note (only worth about $15 at the time) was as big as half a sheet of typing paper!

The twenty-ninth of December was cold and foggy, but we were still enjoying walking around cosmopolitan Milan. My father's diary notes that my parents decided against going to the opera *Norma* by Bellini at La Scala.

What a lost opportunity! Tickets would have been dirt-cheap, and it might have been Maria Callas in the title role. But the opera did not start until 9 PM and we had to catch the train at 8:20 the next morning.

We departed Milan for Rome on the Rapido on December 30, 1955. We had a first-class compartment all to ourselves and were served a four-course lunch on the four-hour trip to Rome. My father's diary notes that the farms we passed looked good. We arrived in Rome at three PM and took a taxi to the Flora Hotel, rooms 123 and 124.

Late afternoon we went shopping. The streets and stores were very crowded. We ate lunch at Necchi's near the Victor Emmanuel monument. The food was very good and the service even better. I remember my mother and father suppressing laughter when my mother raised her spoon, the waiter mistook it for a signal that she wanted a fresh spoon, and substituted spoons while her hand was still in the air.

At midnight on New Year's Eve I was wakened by the noise of people throwing firecrackers out their windows and throwing empty bottles down to smash on the street below. Amazingly, the next morning when we went out for a walk, the sidewalks had already been swept clean.

On New Year's Day 1956 we went to the circus and were about the only people in the audience. We left the Hotel Flora at noon and drove past St. Peter's on our way to the airport. My father saw several other Americans on their way back to Saudi Arabia on the company plane, which left right on time with my mother and me and my sister. My father flew to Beirut on Pan Am, and we all met at the Beirut airport where the company driver, Sayeed, was waiting for us. By then it was almost two AM. Sayeed drove us to the Palm Beach Hotel, where we fell asleep with windows open to the sound of gentle Mediterranean waves on the rocks below.

Grandmother Juna's house at 4410 Garfield Avenue
Photo taken in 2002

Doris, Jack, me in front, my mother,
Ruth holding Linden, Aunt Bonnie and
Grandmother Juna 1954

Aunt Doris and Uncle Jack, Christmas 1954

Juna Porter Wallace

Aunt Doris painted this watercolor of Grandmother Juna's house at 4410 Garfield

Grandmother Grace kept five milk cows on her farm in Effingham, Kansas

My sister Linden and I at Grandmother Grace's farm

5720 Virginia Ave where we rented rooms, photo taken 2002

Commander 9
Kansas City TV 1955

Mother, Linden and me
at the Victor Emmanuel Monument
Rome, December 1955

Ski instructor, Linden, me, and my father, George
Zermatt, December 1955

Mother, Linden, and me in Zermatt
December 1955

January 1956, Lebanon

The next morning we walked down the Beirut Corniche reveling in the mild temperature, the sunshine, and the breeze off the sparkling blue Mediterranean.

After an American breakfast at the hotel, Sayeed drove us down the coast road thirty miles to the town of Sidon. We drove through town, then down a road between orchards of trees with dark-green shiny leaves. "Kumquat trees," my father told us. We stopped in front of a black wrought iron gate in a stone wall. "Couzhou Beit," Sayeed said. He got out and started unloading our luggage. "Couzhou House," my father told us. "This is our new home." An American couple opened the front gates. They introduced themselves to my mother. They were the Sullivans, who had been assigned by TAPline to help us get settled into life in Sidon.

In those days new employees moving overseas were assigned a sponsor from among the employees already living at a jobsite. The sponsor helped the new family get settled in, made sure they had whatever they needed for the first couple of weeks, and made sure they were introduced to other employee families. Many years later, when I went overseas to work in Saudi Arabia, the agency I worked for had the same system. It worked well.

The Sullivans helped my parents get our luggage inside, then Sayeed drove us to their apartment for dinner. Their apartment was very nice, and they told us it had a great view of Sidon harbor from their balcony. I went out on the balcony to take a look, but everything was quite dark.

In those days Lebanese people did not swim or go to the beach for recreation. Outside of Beirut, there were almost no beachfront hotels or resorts. All that has changed—now there are dozens of beachfront hotels in Lebanon.

By the time dinner was over I was exhausted. Sayeed had been patiently waiting with the car and drove us back to our house. I made one more exploration of our house, which I thought was amazingly roomy. There was a small balcony at each second-floor room, and up a narrow flight of concrete steps there was a rooftop terrace overlooking acres of kumquat orchards. It was wonderful! A concrete block wall enclosed the house and a small back yard. Black wrought iron gates opened onto the gravel road in front of the house.

The next morning I woke when our housekeeper, a pleasant young Lebanese woman named Violet, opened the shutters on my balcony doors to let in the bright sunshine and clear Mediterranean air. In the distance were the mountains. The tops of the kumquat trees surrounding the house were like a dark green ocean, and in the distance I could see the foothills of the coastal range mountains.

My father's assignment was to manage the Sidon Training Center (STC), which provided orientation classes on Arab culture, the Arabic language, and ARAMCO operations, for new American employees en route from the USA to Saudi Arabia. The STC also provided basic managerial training for Saudi employees. It was housed in a nice new two-story building with motel-style accommodations for students upstairs, and classrooms, offices, and other facilities downstairs. Among the other facilities were a small auditorium and a photographic darkroom that my father made good use of. During our year in Lebanon he developed and printed hundreds of photos he took on our various excursions.

Many of the recollections I am writing about were triggered by these old photos, all carefully labeled on the back in my mother's neat handwriting. I have always been thankful that my parents kept these photos and equally thankful they labeled them.

The tiny STC "campus" was nicely landscaped and had a sweeping view of the Mediterranean where there was usually a tanker or two loading oil. The town of Sidon was just around a headland to the north, the oil storage tanks and the little refinery were to the south. The coast road ran right by the little campus. There was little traffic on the road; I'd often see men leading donkeys or camels down the road carrying bundles of trade goods, just as their ancestors had for thousands of years.

The campus also had a small snack bar across the lawn from the classroom building.

ARAMCO also had an arrangement with the American University of Beirut (AUB) for Saudi trainee managers to take management courses at the college level.

A week after we arrived in Sidon and had gotten settled in at Couzhou Beit, my father had the company driver, Sayeed, drive us up to Beirut to the AUB campus. While my father discussed business with some of the administrators, my mother, sister, and I strolled around the campus. It had brick buildings, beautifully cared-for trees, shrubs, fountains, and a wonderful view of the Mediterranean. AUB was founded in 1866 by an American named Daniel Bliss as the Syrian Protestant College. In 1920 it changed its educational focus and its name, becoming the American University of Beirut. AUB took the curriculums of the best American private Universities like Harvard and Princeton and modified them by eliminating the requirement to learn Greek and Latin, offering French and English instead. It offered ancient and modern history, physics, chemistry, astronomy, and geology. Most classes were taught in English, but some in Lebanese Arabic.

Over the years the curriculum continued to evolve to fit the needs of young Arab students. In the global student unrest of the 1960s, AUB was caught up even more than American universities with the winds of freedom—discontent with monarchies was just beginning in the Middle East. Then came the Lebanese civil war, whose aftermath left much damage, physical and social.

I resumed my interrupted fourth grade at a tiny one-room elementary school TAPline had set up for employees with school-age kids. There were about ten students, of various ages and grades, or "forms" as our teacher, an English woman, called them. There was only one classroom, just as in rural one-room schools in the USA; the teacher would assign work to students at their level, then would discuss topics with one cohort of kids for an hour, while the rest of us studied quietly at our desks, then she would move to the next age cohort of kids and discuss their lessons with them.

To and from school I rode in a brown '54 Chevy station wagon leased by the company. This was the school bus for four kids: two Norwegian brothers, me, and one American girl in the seventh grade who endlessly complained that she wished she was back home in Dhahran. Every morning on the school bus she would inform us how many days were left until her father transferred back to Dhahran. The rest of the students in the school were Lebanese kids whose parents worked for TAPline. They were enrolled to take advantage of classes taught in English.

In the school bus I always chose the seat just back of the wheel well, which nobody else wanted since legroom was limited. But it had a sliding window that I kept open to the sights and sounds and smells of Sidon as we edged up and down narrow streets picking up the other three kids.

The two Norwegian boys were friendly. Karl-Ivar (pronounced Carl-eevar), the younger of the two brothers, was nine years old, same as me, and we soon became good friends. His father was one of several Norwegian ship pilots hired by TAPline to guide ships to their mooring positions offshore. After the ships were securely anchored, piping was connected, and oil flowed down from the tank farm into the ship. It usually took a week or ten days to fill the tanker with oil. Day by day the ship would sit lower in the water until the red part of her hull was below the level of the water.

At recess we had the wide grassy lawn to play in, with a spectacular view of the Mediterranean. It had a swing set and teeter-totter made of steel pipe by the men in the TAPline machine shops.

One feature of the school was that since we all lived in different parts of Sidon, we didn't see each other after school. It was not like Kansas City where I had the Walker kids downstairs at the house where we lived. In Sidon, when I went home, there were no other kids to play with. But I never felt lonely. I was happy to play games by myself in my room, using toy soldiers and vehicles my parents had bought for me at the Mickey Mouse Toy Store in Beirut. I remember feeling quite happy letting my imagination devise stories about the toys on the carpet in my room while the dark-green kumquat tree leaves rustled in the breeze outside the double doors to the balcony. I was a dreamer then and still am.

One weekend my mother and father took me and my sister along when they went to visit Karl-Ivar's parents. The apartment building they lived in was curved on one end, with the end apartments having a wrap-around balcony, which was pretty cool. We had tea and after a while Karl-Ivar and I went out on the balcony with Borre (Karl-Ivar's older brother) to admire the view. But mostly because Borre wanted to ogle the two women sunbathing in the walled garden behind the building.

Some Saturdays when my father went to the training center darkroom to develop pictures, I would go along with him and spend my time in the lounge beside the snack bar. The lounge had a number of comfortable chairs, a great view, and an upright piano in reasonably good tune. My parents arranged for me to take piano lessons from the Norwegian wife of one of the ship pilots. She was quite a skilled pianist herself (as most European women of her generation were), and she was a patient and kindly instructor, but I had neither talent nor interest in learning the piano, so the lessons soon ended. But still . . . I remember Saturday mornings, when I had the sunny lounge to myself, I would sometimes plunk away on the piano, or read a book, or sit daydreaming.

My father's position entitled him to use the company car and driver for his own purposes on weekends. Sayeed, the Lebanese driver, was punctual, polite, knowledgeable of the Lebanese roads, and very protective of the company car he drove, a brand-new 1956 two-tone green and white Mercury. We spent many weekends sightseeing the various ancient ruins in Lebanon, or shopping in Beirut.

While we were sightseeing at a Phoenician ruin, Sayeed would park the car in the nearest shade and clean it off, inside and out, with a dust cloth.

1956 was a peaceful time in Lebanon. Beirut, just twenty-five miles up the coast from Sidon, was becoming once again what it had been before WWII—"the Paris of the Mediterranean."

Sidon was still a small town whose economy was based on olives, kumquats, lemons, fishing, and boat building. But like many Lebanese cities, its history stretched back three thousand years. It is believed that the people who were later called the Phoenicians migrated to coastal Lebanon from the south, perhaps as far away as Babylon. Why they migrated is unknown, but once they established themselves they became prosperous traders dealing in ceramics and glass, timber, and the purple dye made from murex seashells found along the coast of Lebanon. The purple dye was highly prized during Roman times—wealthy people's togas were usually dyed purple. For a thousand years the Phoenicians from Sidon, Tyre, Byblos, and Tripoli traded all across the Mediterranean, founding cities such as Carthage (in present-day Tunisia) and sailing as far as Spain to trade for Spanish silver. Along with trade they spread arithmetic and writing.

Spring came, the rainy season ended, and the temperatures warmed up to the point we could enjoy the beach. The water was cool, but not cold, and quite clear. Farther out there were rocks with waves breaking on them. There were broken shells on the beach—nothing really good, but we collected many of them anyway. I was fascinated by the shiny black spheres like black BBs on the sand at the water's edge. "That's oil, spilled from the pipes filling the tankers," my father said, pointing to a tanker in the distance.

"Don't step on the oil drops," my mother warned. "It will make a messy black smear on your feet, which is hard to get off."

But of course, my sister and I could not resist touching the fascinating little black orbs. And of course, we got our hands and feet and swimming suits smeared with crude oil.

Most evenings after dinner at Couzhou Beit we'd sit in the living room and my father would read to us. I remember one of the books he read to us was titled *Man-Eaters of Kumaon* by Jim Corbett, who had been a British tea plantation owner in India in the 1930s. In one of the episodes in the book, when a tiger was on the loose in the area, killing livestock and people, the locals would call from village to village "Koo-eee" to indicate the tiger was near. I remember my father laughing as he imitated that call. So then I had to try it. Which I did over and over again at different volumes and intonations until my mother told my father to start reading since she was getting tired of my endless tiger calls.

I still have that faded red-and-white Penguin paperback book on my bookshelf. I remember understanding the author's message that even though he killed tigers from time to time to protect villagers and livestock, tigers were a necessary part of nature and should not be hunted for sport. I tend to agree with that.

There was no TV, but most evenings my father (and most of the other Americans in Lebanon) listened to the BBC World Service radio broadcast from London.

My mother had bought a Victrola record player along with six or eight records on one of our weekend excursions to Beirut. Among the records was a Harry Belafonte record and an Ames Brothers record. She also had a compilation of songs from the current Broadway play, *My Fair Lady*.

Even now, more than sixty years later, I can never hear songs like "I Could Have Danced All Night" or "I've Grown Accustomed to Her Face" without thinking of my room at Couzhou Beit, the deep-green kumquat trees outside, and that music drifting up from downstairs.

Listening to my father read, my mind would fill with images of people and actions from the book, which provided me with a pretty vivid imagination.

This was good since when I was at home with no TV and few books, I spent much time devising an imaginary world, like Charlotte and Emily and Anne Brontë devising their stories in the imaginary world of Gondal in nineteenth-century Yorkshire.

I have always thought I was a more self-sufficient person for having learned early to entertain myself rather than relying on other people or electronics.

My parents and other TAPline employees often held dinner parties in those days. There were only a score of expatriate families living and working in Sidon, and there were few restaurants, no movie theaters, and of course no TV, so people entertained themselves. Dinner parties were good opportunities to put on dressier clothes than day-to-day wear.

Even though children were kept out of the room while the adults conversed and ate dinner, I enjoyed hearing the soothing sound of conversation and laughter from downstairs. In my mind's eye I can see the 1950s furniture of our living room and dining room at Couzhou Beit, and our lamps with their yellow light. I took for granted the way friendships quickly developed among expatriates and suddenly ended when people transferred to other locations.

Bud, a rough-spoken construction foreman, a regular guest at my parents' dinner parties, usually brought a month-old *Los Angeles Times* newspaper for me and my sister, so we could read the "funnies." I found the comic strips like *Li'l Abner* and *Dennis the Menace* boring. There was no *Flash Gordon*, which I would have enjoyed, but there was a *Sir Lancelot* comic strip that was pretty good.

One evening in March my parents were having another of their regular dinner parties. I was told to stay in my room. I could tell who was there by their voices. Mr. and Mrs. Williams, and three different couples with Norwegian-accented English. I recognized the voice of my piano teacher, Mrs. Ludvigsen, and Mr. Tronstad, Karl-Ivar's father. I recognized the Tronstad's huge blue-black Chrysler New Yorker parked in front of the house.

I'd already eaten dinner and was playing with my cars and toy soldiers when I suddenly felt a strange disorientation. I felt as though I was on a ship on the ocean. A couple of my toy soldiers fell over. The light fixture on the ceiling was swaying.

Mother came racing up the stairs with Violet right behind her. She gathered my sister and me up and we were hurried out into the front courtyard where the rest of the adults were standing. There was a lot of tension in the air.

"No sign of fire," Mr. Williams said. "Don't think it's anything at the tank farm or the refinery." The men were worried there had been an explosion at the refinery, but eventually they figured out it had been an earthquake, and we all drifted back inside.

The next morning, riding in the old brown station wagon to school, I saw a number of buildings whose concrete block walls had collapsed.

The rainy season ended and we started going to the beach almost every weekend. The beach was wide, curved, and entirely empty of people. The water was clear and shallow, with no waves. On the sand were surf-smoothed bits of murex shells, broken glass bracelets—usually blue—and occasional pearl-sized shiny black spheres of oil that had leaked from the tanker loading platforms. The beach at Sidon was great fun but much different from the beach I remembered in Saudi Arabia.

The year I was five years old we made many excursions to the beach at Half Moon Bay near Dhahran. I remember very clearly the tall sand dunes sloping down to blue-green Arabian Gulf waters. The sky overhead was a dusty blue, the whole scene was like an abstract painting—sand and sky and sea. No people, no buildings, no vegetation, no signs of animal life for miles in any direction. I have never seen a more dramatic beach than that one on the Arabian Gulf.

In May of 1956 my parents decided on a short vacation to visit Jerusalem and Petra in Jordan.

The ninth of May was clear and breezy. Sayeed drove us to Beirut Airport, where we caught a plane for the short hop to Amman, Jordan, which turned out to be a very nice city—not quite as cosmopolitan as Beirut, but very nice. The people were friendly. We spent that afternoon sightseeing in Amman, and the next day flew to Jerusalem and checked in to the Ambassador Hotel. My father arranged for a car and English-speaking guide to show us around Jerusalem.

To me, the Palm Sunday route looked like any other dusty Middle Eastern road. The Mount of Olives was nice, with its olive trees and dusty shade. From the top of the hill we walked down to the garden of Gethsemane. "Which means 'olive press,'" my father read to us from his guidebook. "Jesus and his followers came here often. It was a nice place to rest." It was OK, I thought, but not much of a garden. My grandmother's garden in Kansas was a real garden; this was a shady grove of trees. "Jesus is thought to have prayed here just before he was arrested by the Roman soldiers."

"Why?" my sister asked.

"He was breaking the law by promoting a religion different from the official religion of Rome. This area was part of the Roman Empire at the time."

The driver took us down to Lion's Gate and dropped us off. "Lion's Gate," my father read, "was one of the gates of old Jerusalem in Roman times. It was known as Stephen's Gate until the carved lions were installed by Suleiman the Magnificent, the Ottoman emperor, in 1517 to celebrate his victory over the Mamluks."

I nodded.

"I'll give you more of the history later, but now we should start walking." So we started up the stone street that was the Via Dolorosa. "Via Dolorosa in Latin means 'way of sorrow,'" my father read. "It's the route Jesus is said to have taken to a hill, Golgotha, to be executed." It looked pretty ordinary to me. "The stations of the cross have conflicting interpretations in different sects of Christianity, and the exact location of the Via Dolorosa isn't known for sure. They are mentioned in the books of Matthew, John, and James." My father liked to read us things from the guidebook. Our guide seemed OK with having my father explain things to us. "The last four stations are inside the Church of the Holy Sepulchre, which is where we are going next."

My mother borrowed the guidebook and began leafing through it. "Here's the fifth station," she said. "Commemorates Jesus meeting Simon of Cyrene, who carried his cross for him for a while." She stepped aside to let a cart pass. "Noted in Matthew, repeated in Mark and Luke, but not in John."

"Those stories aren't accurate," my father laughed. "They're based on verbal accounts, some fictional, written down long after the fact, copied and recopied by hand, then fifteen hundred years of embellishment. It's best just to read the bible for its sense of the Middle East as it was two thousand years ago. And to learn from the positive aspects of the legends."

"What's a sepulchre?" my sister asked.

"It's an old word for a place where a dead body is brought before it is buried. Jesus's body was brought here," my father told her.

We stopped at the place of the Ascension for a moment. There wasn't much to see, so we moved on to the big tile courtyard of the Dome of the Rock Mosque. Inside it was a big open octagonal room with windows above. The light was beautiful on the intricate filigree tile work along the walls. At the front door was a pile of slip-on leather sandals. We each found two sandals and slipped them over our shoes. "Usually people remove their shoes when entering a mosque," my father explained. "But there are so many tourists coming to this one that they allow you to wear these indoor slippers over your shoes."

We wandered around for a few moments. The place felt big and airy, calm and very pleasant. There were a handful of people here and there, including a man saying his prayers near the wall aligned with the direction of Mecca. The churches we'd visited seemed dark and confined compared to this mosque.

That afternoon we drove to Bethlehem, made a quick visit to the Church of the Nativity, then stopped in a gift shop and bought a half dozen souvenir Bibles with inlaid mother-of-pearl patterns on front and back. Then the driver took us to the American Colony Hotel, where we had a very nice afternoon tea in the shady garden. The shortbread cookies were nice, but I really didn't think cucumbers made good sandwich filling. As evening came we returned to the Ambassador Hotel, ate dinner in the dining room, and retired for the night in our rooms on the fourth floor.

The next morning the hired car drove us out to the archeological excavations at Jericho. We viewed some deep holes in the ground where crude brick walls stood exposed. Then we drove to the Dead Sea, took off our shoes, and waded in it. "The water is so salty you can easily float in it," my father told us. "But we don't have time for you to swim—just wade, then we'll go back to the hotel." I was disappointed we hadn't gone for a swim, but back at the hotel I was glad to rinse the itchy salt off my feet.

The next day we breakfasted as soon as the dining room opened, then took a taxi to the airport and boarded an old DC-3 for the short flight to Ma'an, where the ruins of Petra were.

The DC-3's steeply slanted aisle, worn seat covers, and old wool window curtains seemed very familiar. Some of my earliest memories are of long flights with my parents on MATS (Military Air Transport System) DC-3s. While my father was on active duty we could fly space-available for free.

The plane flew south over desert and soon descended to a single asphalt airstrip near several stone buildings. The entire landscape was shades of tan and ochre. Jordanian guides greeted us and the other tourists, and we followed them out to a horse corral shaded by a woven rattan roof.

We were each mounted on a horse, which was led by a Jordanian horse handler. I had a horse of my own, which I thought was pretty neat. My mother carried my sister ahead of her on the saddle of her horse. The guide walked beside my father, describing things. His English was quite good, with a strong Cockney accent. We crossed an open rocky area then entered a narrow opening in a rocky cliff. After a short way, we stopped in a wide area, shaded from the sun, while the guide explained:

"Two thousand years ago this rocky area with the narrow entrance was settled by a tribe called the Nabateans that historians believe migrated north from Arabia, perhaps from as far south as Babylon. The climate was cooler and wetter two thousand years ago, so agriculture was possible here. But this location was also easily defended from attack, and it was a watering point for caravans coming up the Red Sea coast from Yemen bringing spices that the Phoenicians then traded all around the Mediterranean. The Nabateans settled here in the sixth century BC, became prosperous, and absorbed the local Aramaic culture that overlaid their Arab roots."

We moved on; it was silent and cool in the narrow channel. I repressed an urge to let out a shout just to hear it echo. Then we reached a wide spot in the passage and stopped in front of the ornate carved temple, which I recognized from the tourist posters back in Amman. "This is called the 'Treasury' or 'Pharaoh's tomb,'" the guide explained. "Why it has those names, no one knows, but it is likely they were made up by European explorers a hundred years ago. This structure was actually probably a tomb for a Nabatean king."

Farther along we came out into the open. The bare mountains around us had none of the red and white color of the rock in the narrow passage. The horsemen led us to a shaded spot out of the heat and glare of the sun. "This amphitheater was built in Roman times," the guide explained. "Petra was a very defensible spot and located at the junction of the camel caravan route from Yemen to the caravan route from Alexandria to Damascus."

We dismounted and walked around the amphitheater for a while, then got back on our horses for the return trip to the airport.

At the airport police station I stood in the shade looking out to the southwest at endless desert. The caravans had to cross that desert to bring trade goods. I imagined what it must have been like to take those long caravan trips. And what Petra had been like before the Roman army came and during the Roman occupation. I wondered why Nabatean Petra declined in importance and disappeared entirely from history after the collapse of the Roman empire, until European explorers rediscovered the ruins in the early nineteenth century.

My father came out of the terminal building looking rather unhappy. "Our flight is delayed. The plane hasn't even left Jerusalem yet. Some kind of mechanical problem. Supposed to be here in an hour."

My mother told him not to get upset; this was a good place to wait for the plane. My father commiserated with the other tourists—two British ladies and an older American couple from Cairo—then seated himself and read his guidebook. I rather enjoyed waiting on the bench on the shaded porch, daydreaming about ancient empires. It was entirely silent.

I daydreamed of the ancient tribes that had lived here, died here, generation after generation, their population dwindling until only ghosts inhabited the tombs and the amphitheater. I thought for a moment of the silent ghosts in the shadows in my grandmother's barn on the other side of the world.

The plane eventually arrived and we returned to Jerusalem and the comforts of the Ambassador Hotel. At dinner that night my father read from the guidebook, "The ancient Nabatean city of Petra was not only on the trade route from Saudi Arabia, actually Yemen, to the Mediterranean ports, but also on the east–west trade route from Alexandria to Damascus and on to Europe."

"Or from Damascus . . ."

"The guide pronounced it Damash," I interjected.

He smiled. "Arabic into French and back to Arabic," my father laughed. "Yes, trade route to Damash and on to Palmyra and south to the Arabian Gulf."

"You've been to the ruins of Palmyra," my mother told me. "It was cold."

I was only five years old when we went to Palmyra, and while I do have some memories of that long-ago trip, it is more likely that I have seen the slides my parents took on that trip and formed them into memories. With the passage of time, photos become our memories.

The next morning we caught our flight back to Beirut, where Sayeed met us with the car and drove us home to Couzhou Beit.

"The Jordanians are certainly friendly people," my mother said. "Their features and dress are clearly different from both the Saudis and the Lebanese."

As we approached the vegetable stand in Damour, Sayeed glanced inquiringly at my father.

"Not today, Sayeed. Let's go straight to Sidon."

On the eleventh of July we embarked on a sightseeing trip to Baalbek and afterward to Beirut, where we would spend the night at the Eden Roc Hotel. Sayeed drove us up the winding coast road. As always we passed women walking home from the village well, a jug of water balanced on their heads. They made it look effortless, so I resolved to try it myself one day at home.

"The trees on those terraced fields," my father said, pointing. "I think they are apple trees, and I've seen olive trees and what I think are fig trees." He glanced at my mother and sister and me in the back seat. "Those terraces are only about twenty feet wide, and the rock retaining wall was probably built by hand with donkeys to carry to stones." He shook his head. "So much work compared to American farms with their big flat fields. We've got it pretty easy."

The Roman ruins at Baalbek are the best in Lebanon. We spent four hours roaming over the site. First we ate the box lunch we had brought with us while my father read to us from his ever-present guidebook.

"This town grew up because it had good water and was on the caravan route from Tyre to Palmyra. Before the Romans this city was part of a federation of city-states, and the gods of this area were Baal and Astarte. Then about year zero the Romans tore down the original temples and built these temples for the worship of Jupiter and Atargatis, Jupiter's consort. They eliminated old temples and built temples to their gods to reinforce their political and military presence here. This town protected, and taxed, the trade caravans. And it formed the eastern line of defense of the Roman Empire."

We started walking through the ruins. "See this stone carving of a lion's head?" my mother said with a smile. "We were here in 1949. We have a photo of the three of us standing right here."

I had no memory of that visit.

"Where was I?" my sister asked.

"You weren't born yet."

I explored the ruined temples by myself. After a while I sat down in the cool shadow of the base of one of the ancient pillars and daydreamed about the Roman Empire, the greatest empire the world had ever seen. I knew the empire had fallen apart due to Roman infighting, Christian insurrection, and external barbarian assaults.

Daydreamer

Even at age ten I could see the irony in barbarians destroying the very thing they wanted most—all the luxuries and advantages of Roman culture.

I walked to the end of the colonnade and stood facing the hot desert wind from the Bekaa Valley and thought of the tribal people out in the vast desert. Tribal people who still lived their short lives knowing nothing more than their own tribe and the caravan routes between oases. In that direction across the desert was another ruined city, Palmyra. There Queen Zenobia defied Roman authority for a while; but soon she was captured and Palmyra declined into insignificance. Two thousand years of lives lived and forgotten. The hot desert wind on my face hinted at their ghosts.

Late afternoon we got in the car and started back to Beirut. Going over the mountains, the air got noticeably cooler, and soon the lights of Beirut were spread out before us.

The Eden Roc Hotel was right on the Corniche in Beirut. It was a very 1950s stylish hotel, built of concrete and glass. Our rooms had a great view of the Mediterranean. The swimming pool was elevated above the rocks below, so sunbathers had an unrestricted view of the Mediterranean Sea. Before dinner I wandered out to the handrail and watched the waves breaking gently on the rocks below. The rooms were very modern, very comfortable, and the sound of the waves coming in through the open windows was wonderful.

The next day, after a leisurely American breakfast on the patio by the swimming pool, Sayeed drove us back down the coast road to Sidon. At Damour we stopped, as we often did, for a bottle of orange soda, which we drank through a straw. My mother decided to buy a set of woven rattan baskets and four rattan footstools from the weaving shop next to the little cafe.

One Friday night in mid-July my father read to us from a Harold Lamb book titled *Suleiman the Magnificent*. "This about the sixteenth-century Ottoman Turk emperor named Suleiman," he told us. "Tomorrow we are going to see Beit ed-Dine, the former

Ottoman Turk palace. It's now a historic site. Another part of it is the president of Lebanon's summer palace."

Early the next morning, my sister and I piled into the back seat of the Mercury with our mother. My father and Sayeed in the front seat, we started north on the coast road just at daybreak. Mr. and Mrs. Luckenbaugh followed us in their own car. A few kilometers past Damour we turned inland, going up a narrow winding road up and down the hillsides, past terraced fields only ten feet wide. "Millet and chickpeas in these little fields," my father told us. "And there are olive trees, and that's a little grape vineyard over there."

We stopped for brunch at a little Lebanese restaurant near Beit ed-Dine, where we had bread and jam with tea, then paid a fee and were allowed inside the former palace. I was unimpressed, and I sensed my mother and father were not impressed either. Within an hour we were back in the car and on to the town of Zahle. As we wound through the hills I caught glimpses of the desert past the mountains to the east. The mountains here were not as tall as the mountains east of Beirut, where the cedars of Lebanon are, but they were scenic. We stopped several times at roadside overlooks to stretch our legs and for my father to take a picture.

At Zahle we ate lunch in a local restaurant—built into one of the many caves in this part of the mountains. It was a little gloomy, but the service was good and the food was quite good. We didn't eat the salad, but the tabouli, bread, and roasted lamb were great. I never liked the sour cream garnish, but my parents did. The restaurant's wooden tables and rattan chairs weren't elegant, but it was cool and quiet.

Then we parked the car and walked down the streets of Zahle to the waterfall and took some pictures.

Then back to Sidon.

On Friday night, the twenty-sixth of July, my parents were having another dinner party. My sister and I ate upstairs at the table and four chairs in the anteroom at the head of the stairs. The guests and our parents had dinner downstairs. Violet brought a tray with our food up to us and departed to do kitchen work. The guests all arrived on time.

That was another lesson I learned without being taught—to be punctual. My parents were very punctual people, and I overheard them tell each other more than once how irritating it was to deal with people who were not.

We had been told at school that day that President Nasser of Egypt had nationalized the Suez Canal. My parents had talked about cancelling the party, but decided to proceed with it.

I could hear six or seven voices, the clinking of glassware, an occasional laugh. But the laughs were a bit strained.

From time to time the tone of the murmur would change to sadness, sometimes fear, and I knew the adults were discussing the simultaneous British and French invasion of Suez and the Israeli invasion of the Sinai.

"Nasser can't last," someone said. "Even with all that Soviet military equipment."

Violet came in to clear my dinner tray. She stood for a moment looking at the sunset glow of dusty orange under low clouds, the sheen of silver off the Mediterranean, the thin dark shadows of the tankers at the loading platform. She was frowning. After a time she turned. "Open?" she asked in English.

"Yes, open," I told her. She left the drapes open and departed. My second-floor room felt like a ship on a deep-green kumquat forest. After she had gone, I set aside my book, Jules Verne's *For the Flag*, and watched the sunset from my balcony.

Raised voices came from the living room. I heard a strident shout, a hoarse response, and then silence. The front door opened and closed. I peered out the front window and saw a man hurry down the tile walkway, bang the wrought iron gate open, get in his car, and speed away. I crept out to the bannister at the head of the stairs.

The crystal click and tap of glasses and teacups had resumed.

". . . didn't think he'd take it so . . ."

"Appalling!" snapped Miss Martin, her full British classroom voice easily carrying up the stairs. "Apparently Mr. Borreson doesn't realize how crucial Suez is to getting oil to Europe and Britain. Our troops and the French need to be here . . ."

"Why the Israelis?" someone asked her, and I could imagine the disdain she used in the classroom when she didn't know the answer. "They are our allies."

"Maybe," someone said.

I heard my father in a placating tone say, "Bengt's just worried about his family. He'll be back to normal tomorrow."

"Yeah, he will." That was Bud Williams, from oil operations, the guy who sometimes brought a copy of the *Los Angeles Times* for us to read. "He'll be back to normal tomorrow because he and his family will be on the flight to Athens tomorrow. Bengt drove up to Beirut yesterday and got the tickets. He's taking his family back to Norway."

"Nasser's got everybody worried," someone said. "President Eisenhower wants to help President Chamoun's government here in Lebanon, but the Israeli invasion of the Sinai is really going to make that difficult."

"And of course the Israeli lobby will force the US congress to support Israel no matter how wrong it is." That was Mr. Barber, the assistant for industrial operations from the American embassy.

Mr. James laughed a strange laugh. "An American puppet is better than a Soviet puppet. Right?"

I envisioned a man-sized marionette in blue and gold uniform.

I crept back to my room and got into bed to read more in my Jules Verne book.

On the twenty-ninth of July at breakfast my father told my sister and me we were going to take a day trip to Eagle's Eyrie. As I ate my chicken soup and salad with yogurt I imagined a mountaintop with big eagles perched all around, some soaring down into the valley below. "Some acquaintances of ours live there and have invited us for coffee," my mother said.

Sayeed brought the car around promptly at nine. We piled in and drove north on the coast road for an hour. In the back seat, I liked sitting on the left side so that I would have a great view of the familiar coastline. At Damour we stopped to, as my father said on every trip, "stretch our legs." My mother browsed the melon and vegetable stand

and wandered over to the basket shop. I walked over to the edge of the road and stared down the rugged drop to the Mediterranean.

Back in the car we drove up a winding road into the tree-covered mountains. As we drove up the winding mountain road the air became cooler. My father, as usual, pointed out what was growing in the narrow fields.

My father grew up on a farm and never outgrew the habit of noticing what local farmers were growing.

"This would be very arid rocky soil if it weren't for the rain the coastal winds bring. Once we get to the top of the coastal range and start down the other side, it is a lot drier."

"Do the Bushakras have olive groves, or goat herds?" my mother asked. "How do they make a living?"

"I don't know," he said. "We'll find out."

Mr. and Mrs. Bushakra met us at the entrance to their estate, a stone archway. She was an American, he was Lebanese. After greetings all around we walked the last hundred yards to their comfortable home overlooking the valley. A silent girl in Druze dress served coffee. My sister and I were each given a glass of Kaki Kola with no ice.

After a while I wandered off to explore. The house was on top of a hill with a nice view. It was surrounded by olive groves, which I didn't find very interesting. The olive trees had thin pale-green leaves, completely different from the dark-green leaves of the kumquat trees around our house in Sidon. Back inside I sat on the carpet near the little wooden table that held the tea service on its tray.

Mr. Bushakra had taken my father out to show him around the olive grove and grape arbors.

"Go home?" Mrs. Bushakra smiled at my mother's question. "Back to New York? Or to Pennsylvania where my family once lived? No. My family is gone now, so I have no reason to go back to Pennsylvania. Fuad and I lived in New York for over twelve years, and we liked it, but that was twenty years ago. This has been our home, and our family, since 1937." She made a gesture with her hand that took in their hilltop, the valley, the town of Ammateur, and all of Druze Mountain. "My family is everyone in this valley and the next. And I like being this close to the land. I never had that as an adult in New York or as a child in Pennsylvania."

My mother said rather wistfully, "I want to be close to the land too. With the political unrest here and the Israeli threat . . . maybe now is the time to go back to the States. George doesn't really want to go—he's put so much work into the training center. But the company is considering divesting itself of the refinery and oil terminal at Sidon. Too much political and military uncertainty."

"I had not heard that." Mrs. Bushakra poured more coffee. "But I seldom hear news of anything beyond this valley."

Mr. Bushakra and my father returned. Mr. Bushakra smiled and shrugged. "War has come to Druze Mountain before. The Turks, the French, now the Israelis." His wife poured a minute amount of coffee into his cup. He smiled at her, then at the cup of coffee. "I have the kindness of my family, and of Allah." He smiled again. "We will survive. Roots must go deep to survive in this rocky soil."

Mrs. Bushakra, Winnie, as she told my parents she liked to be called, went on to describe their crossing by ship from New York to Beirut. "We brought everything for this house, including a generator," she laughed. "The first port we saw on this coast was Tel Aviv and then Jaffa. As our ship travelled up the coast I picked out Tyre then Sidon . . ."

"Could you see the old Phoenician fort out on the rocks at Sidon?" I piped up. "And the lighthouse?"

She smiled. "Do you know what kinds of things the ancient Phoenicians traded all around the Mediterranean?"

"Purple dye," I said. "The Romans used it for their togas."

"What was the dye made from?"

"Sea shells."

Daydreamer

"That's right—murex shells, a species of conch. The Phoenicians also traded fir and cedar wood for buildings and for ship building." Winnie raised her hand to her mouth. "I shouldn't be chattering on . . ."

My parents assured her it was fascinating, and she told us a little more about coming to this hilltop, building this house, building relationships with Fuad's extended family. Then she said, "I'd like to give you a small gift."

She left the room and came back in a moment with a book, which she gave to my mother. "I wrote that memoir five years ago." She shrugged a little. "Just to be able to remember when I first came to Lebanon. Now I find it hard to believe I have been here for fifteen years."

My parents thanked her for the book and for a pleasant visit, and soon we departed for the drive back to Sidon.

At home I looked in the book. Winnie had inscribed it: *To recall our pleasant afternoon together at Eagle's Eyrie, July 29, 1956.*

Wow, I thought, I've met someone who wrote a book. A real author.

I still have that book. It is a nicely told reminiscence of Winnie and Fuad's emigration to their mountaintop in Lebanon and getting settled into their extended family.

It describes a time that no longer exists. I wonder if Eagle's Eyrie is still standing today? And if the current owners know anything of Winnie and Fuad?

One weekend in August we drove south to Tyre, whose name, as Mrs. Bushakra had told us, is derived from the Arabic word for rock, tsur.

I'm sure Sayeed wondered why my father had chosen for us to stay at an older, but quite nice, hotel called The Bird Hotel. The lobby was clean and 1940s European modern. We took a creaking ancient elevator up to the second floor. Our two rooms had balconies overlooking a pedestrian street behind the hotel. I don't remember where we ate dinner, but I do remember that afterward, on impulse, we stopped in a movie theater and watched *Land of the Pharaohs*, subtitled in Arabic. It was a bad print of the film, all red-tinted.

I didn't think Jack Hawkins made a very convincing Pharaoh. Joan Collins as an Egyptian had the audience chuckling - who knows what the Arabic subtitles were translating her dialogue into. But I remember to this day the scene where slaves are rolling big blocks of stone on wooden rollers as they build a pyramid. One slave gets his clothing caught and is pulled under the rollers. My sister hid her face. The final scene with the big blocks of stone sliding into place, trapping Joan Collins with the dead Pharaoh, was also suitably horrific.

Back at the hotel we opened the balcony doors. The scent of coffee beans roasting over wood-fired braziers drifted up in the calm night air. Bats flitted above. There was also the scent of shawarma roasting, and Latakia tobacco from the hubble-bubbles men were smoking.

In the dim glow from the one ceiling light in the hotel room, my father read to us from his guidebook. "Ancient Tyre was the biggest and most influential city-state of the Phoenicians three thousand years ago. The Phoenician people were Canaanites who settled in this area five millennia ago. Anthropologists believe they were pushed into the coastal region by the expansion of the Assyrian Empire. Ships from Tyre sailed the length of the Mediterranean, trading. One of their outposts, where they traded for African wheat, became the city of Carthage in present-day Tunisia. Carthage grew to be so big and powerful that by 300 BC Rome decided it was threatening the dominance of the Roman Empire and so decided to destroy it. Three Punic wars resulted, and even though Hannibal and his Carthaginian army crossed the Mediterranean and pushed the Roman armies back, in the end they lost the wars. In 146 BC the Roman army arrived in Carthage and destroyed the city. If Carthage had won those wars instead of Rome, history would have taken a very different course."

In 19 BCE Virgil wrote his classic story the Aeneid *in which Aeneas comes to Carthage and meets Dido, the legendary queen and founder of Carthage. In the nineteenth century Gustave Flaubert visited the ruins of Carthage and wrote a book called* Salammbo. *The title character is a fictitious queen of Carthage modeled on Dido. The book, published in 1862 and very popular in its day, still reads fairly well.*

The next day we went to the ruins, which were on the rocky coast overlooking a windswept Mediterranean. We clambered around the stone blocks of temple foundations and a colonnade. It was a windy day; there were tiny whitecaps on the waves rolling in from the west.

"These are Roman ruins," my father told us, "not Phoenician. Tyre, as a trading city, was at its peak a thousand years before these temples were built."

I wandered off over the sun-warmed stone blocks. A thousand years? I could not envision that length of time. And three thousand years? That length of time was even more fantastic. I felt a mystic aura about these ancient ruins overlooking the sea, and all the people who had lived their lives, died, and been forgotten in three thousand years.

My father read more from the guidebook. "About 1100 BC, Assyria became an aggressive military empire. They conquered the Hittites in present-day Turkey and pushed the Babylonians back south. They fought with the nomads of the Syrian Desert and 'the people of the sea,' namely, the Phoenicians. When the Assyrians took over Damascus and Aleppo, the people of Tyre were happy, since they now faced less trade competition from those great cities."

He showed me an illustration in the guidebook—a stone Assyrian winged bull with the bearded head of a man. It was awe-inspiring, even across three thousand years of time.

"The capitol of the Assyrian Empire was Nineveh, near present-day Tikrit, Iraq. At first Assyria expanded in all directions, but by about 1200 BC, both Assyria and the Egyptian empire stopped expanding due to internal problems. The Phoenician city-states were left autonomous since they were a long way from Alexandria and from Nineveh. Both Egypt and the Assyrians wanted the things the Phoenicians could import and sell them—gold, silver, copper, pottery, glass, and luxury goods. The Phoenicians received trade goods coming overland along the caravan routes and sold them in Cyprus and all along the Eastern Mediterranean. The Phoenician city-states of Tyre, Sidon, Beirut, Byblos, and Tripoli increased their Mediterranean trading. Over the course of centuries they built up a huge trading network, with trading outposts on the coast all over the Med, all the way to Spain."

"Why go so far?" I asked.

"There was silver in Spain—silver mines inland from present-day Cadiz—and silver was always in demand. Luxuries are always in demand; they make the best trade goods, along with pottery and glass. Phoenicians also manufactured artworks in the styles their customers wanted, Egyptian for the Egyptians."

"And purple dye," I added.

"Yes. It was an amazing empire . . . no, empire is not the right word . . . the ancient Phoenicians brought their culture across the entire Mediterranean without invasions, armies, or political control. It's amazing." My father set his book aside and lost himself in thought for a time. I was still immersed in images of those ancient travels across the Mediterranean in sailboats. Like the Vikings two thousand years later, although the North Sea was a lot colder and stormier than the placid Mediterranean.

One Friday night in mid-August my father announced to my sister and me that we were going to drive up to Tripoli Saturday morning, spend the day sightseeing, spend the night in a hotel there, and come back to Sidon on Sunday. It was 120 kilometers from Sidon to Tripoli, which made for a long trip since you had to drive through Beirut to continue north. I dozed and daydreamed the long hours. Once we got to Tripoli we went to the crusader castle ruin first.

Once again my father read from his ever-present guidebook. "Some say Tripoli was not an original Phoenician city; it was founded by other people. It is the city farthest north in Lebanon. The Christian crusaders burned a big library here when they invaded and took over. Raymond St. Gilles, a French knight from Toulouse, was chief among them. He and his invading army killed many of the people here. He died here in 1104 after three marriages and many broken treaties. Typical crusader." I could tell that my father was in a sour mood that day, so I got permission from my mother and went off to explore on my own. Half an hour later, when I returned from climbing around the ruins, my father seemed to be in a better mood. He took up his account of Raymond the Crusader.

"After Raymond died the remaining crusaders built up this citadel and named it after him. Before the Christians took over, Tripoli—under Arab rule—was the port city for Damascus. In addition to imported trade goods, Tripoli exported oranges and other fruit to Europe."

We got back in the car, drove back to Beirut, and checked into the Hotel St. Georges. The subtle Mediterranean autumn had arrived, the air was cooler, the sunshine a bit brighter. We were exhausted after a long day of driving and sightseeing so went to bed early. The next day we ate croissants and English tea at a sidewalk cafe, then we went window shopping at the clothing and household goods stores, much of the merchandise imported from France. We had a late lunch in a restaurant overlooking the bright blue Mediterranean. The menu was in French, and my mother enjoyed practicing what remained of her high school French with the waiters and waitresses who spoke French in addition to English and Arabic.

After lunch my father had Sayeed drive us to the Friendly Bookstore. As always the front door stood open to the mimosa-shaded sidewalk where sparrows flitted and chirped. Inside, it smelled of new books and of Mr. Habib's hair oil and Latakia pipe tobacco. He was a friendly, quiet man, always sitting behind the counter reading a book. Sometimes a book in French, sometimes Arabic, sometimes English.

We visited the Friendly Bookstore many times during our year in Lebanon. I can easily remember Mr. Habib, always reading, always dressed in a brown sleeveless sweater with his shirt buttoned all the way to the collar.

The store was arranged so that books and magazines were grouped by language: Arabic, French, and English. I went to the English section and scanned the bottom row, where I knew he put the British editions of H.G. Wells and Jules Verne.

I read for a while.

Down the aisle I noticed my mother carefully examining a book she'd pulled from the shelf. I could see she had decided to buy it. She glanced out the window at my father sitting on the bench under a mimosa tree smoking a cigar. She quickly went to the counter and gave Mr. Habib a blue Lebanese five-pound note. He wrapped the book in brown paper tied with a string, and she quickly put it in her purse.

Next we made a stop at the new campus of the American Community School (ACS), which offered a western-style kindergarten through high school education. It was founded in 1905, but it was only with the construction of the new campus, right on the Corniche in Beirut, that ACS became a true international school. The new campus was built with ARAMCO money, and many of the three hundred students were children of ARAMCO employees attending boarding school while their parents lived and worked in the oil fields of Saudi Arabia.

My parents probably thought of having me attend ACS for junior high and high school.

Years later I read the reminiscences of students and faculty who had been at ACS in the 1950s through 1980s (Al Mashriq press, titled When . . . Not If, Fill the Bathtub, *and* Anything but Ordinary, *released in 2010, 2011, and 2013, respectively).*

I have often speculated on how different a person I might have been if we'd stayed in Lebanon, and I'd attended ACS.

On September 23 we had Sayeed drive us north on the coast highway to Byblos, another Phoenician trading city now gaining prominence as a beachfront resort with a number of new hotels catering to European tourists. We had lunch at a beachfront restaurant then walked the ancient streets of the city to Byblos crusader castle.

"Byblos has a long history," my father read to us, "dating back to Phoenician days, but it is not as famous as Tyre or Tripoli. It is thought by some historians that boats with keels were first devised in Phoenician Byblos." My father illustrated with his hands how a sailboat's sail and keel push at angles to each other, which allows a boat to travel in many directions, not just downwind. "That boat design is what allowed the Phoenicians to sail all across the Mediterranean. A Greek man, Philo of Byblos, who lived from AD

64 to AD 141, wrote a history of the Phoenicians, and since he wrote it in Greek instead of Arabic, the Romans could translate it and took it to be fact, even though he probably made most of it up. He was writing about things that happened eight hundred years before he was born. In Byblos the main gods were Melqart and his wife Astarte."

"What happened to the Phoenicians?" I asked.

"The Phoenicians are still here. They are the Lebanese people. This castle was abandoned in about 1200 AD after the Muslims threw the Christian invaders out and warfare ceased."

"Why did the crusaders invade Lebanon in the first place?"

"They were Christians and wanted to own Jerusalem since that's where Christianity began. And they did own it for a while. But the Europeans tended to treat the local people harshly; in fact, they used slave labor to build these castles, so eventually the Arabs ran them out. You remember the story of Richard the Lion-Hearted? Well, he was one of the crusaders." My father thumbed through his guidebook. "The last battle was in 1187 when Saladin finally defeated the Christians."

"Saladin was the leader of the Arab armies," the normally silent Linden said. "It said so in the book." Back in Sidon, our father had been reading a book to us called *Knight Crusader*.

"That's right," my father said. "After the defeat of the Christians, Byblos became a center of commerce and later part of the Ottoman Empire . . ."

"The Turks," I interjected again.

"Right," my father said. "Let's walk around the castle ruins another ten minutes, then we need to start back to Sidon."

On the twenty-first of October we drove up to Beirut. My father had scheduled a meeting with the administrator of the American University of Beirut. But first we stopped by the Beirut racetrack. In 1950s Beirut gambling was legal—there was a casino and there was a horseracing track. My father liked horses—he'd been a horse rider since childhood, so he enjoyed looking at the horses—but he was not a gambler, so we left after watching a couple of races. Sayeed drove us to the AUB campus. While my father attended his meeting, my mother, sister, and I walked around campus. It was very beautiful among the olive trees and sandstone fountains.

After a while my father rejoined us and we walked through the campus to the street. I could tell by the smile on his face that my father had had a successful meeting.

"This is very nice," my mother said.

"The Phoenicians were not great scholars," he told us, "but the Arabs were. Damascus was a great center of learning in the middle ages. The Arabs were astronomers among other things. Many of the stars were named by Arab astronomers: Deneb, Algol, Aldebaran."

Just off campus was a teashop where we drank sweet Lebanese tea served in little cups made of thick glass. We ate French bread, with a little bowl of black vinegar for dipping, goat's milk cheese, and dark-red olives in clear yellow oil.

Then back to Sidon.

Winter was coming and the nights were often chilly. Most evenings we'd stay near the big gas heater in the living room. A couple of weeks ago, on a visit to Beirut, I'd seen a plastic model sailing ship in Mickey Mouse Toy Store, and my father had bought it for me. He'd also bought some Duco cement and some paint, which we would need to complete the model.

I got the box out and my father and I set to work assembling the tiny sailing ship model. I had never had much interest in assembling plastic models, but this time it was fun. My father seemed to enjoy it too. As we worked he described conditions in the British Royal Navy at the time of Lord Nelson—which sounded pretty horrific (he'd toured a ship of the line on display at the wharves in London years ago). "Nelson built the British Navy and the British Navy built the British Empire," he told me.

While the LP gas stove hissed cheerfully I laid out all the plastic pieces of the model on the dining room table and we began assembling it. We finished gluing it together that evening and painted it the next evening. I remember one of the colors was Prussian blue, which we used to paint the ocean. We added a tiny drop of white paint to the tops of some of the plastic waves to represent white caps.

That small model ship, dusty and with parts of the rigging hanging unglued, sits on my desk as I am writing this. I'm glad my parents kept that model ship all these years. And the books my father read to us. Because without them I would likely not have remembered those evenings so clearly.

On another chilly evening my parents reminisced about an earlier trip they had taken to Beirut and to Damascus. In 1949 my father was still in the Air Force, on active duty at Dhahran Air Base, where he and my mother and I had lived for a year (my sister had not been born yet). In July he had taken a short vacation, and the three of us flew on a military DC-3 to Beirut. We stayed at the St. Georges Hotel in Beirut, right on the Corniche, overlooking the Mediterranean. We'd hired a car and visited Baalbek and AUB, where a few Saudi students were attending classes. The American Air Force training mission at Dhahran was responsible for identifying Saudi students with good potential and sending them to AUB. My father's diary says we spent two nights in the guest suite at AUB in "Pinkstones," a building overlooking the playing field. The room was luxurious and the campus was beautiful.

The years from 1945 to 1995 were perhaps the best days for modern Lebanon. French Colonial days were over, WWII was over, the British were gone, the economy was growing, and Beirut was forming itself into the most sophisticated city in the Middle East. Cairo and Damascus were bigger, but they did not have the élan of French-flavored, coastal Beirut.
All this beauty was destroyed by the 1995–2010 civil war in Lebanon.

After their reminiscence, my parents fell silent for a moment. Then my mother said slowly, "I know you want to stay here, but if the political situation gets worse, and of course if TAPline closes the training center, we should move on to the next phase of our lives."

My father said nothing.

We drove past the teashop and vegetable market in the village of Damour. My father motioned Sayeed to keep going. In all our previous trips to Beirut we'd stop there at evening. We'd sit on hand-woven cane chairs at a wooden table and watch the orange ball of the sun sink into the Mediterranean. The owner would start the generator just for us, and the three bare light bulbs would cast a stark light over the vegetable baskets where the girls were putting the produce away for the night. I'd drink lemon cola while my parents drank sweet tea in small thick glasses.

Afterward, on the road again, my mother would almost always hum "Chanson D'Amour," which would get a chuckle from my father. But this evening she was silent.

I drowsed in the back seat until the lights of the tankers and the oil refinery come into view. I imagined the ships were spaceships; the refinery was an outpost on a planet orbiting the red star Antares.

December 1 was my father's birthday. As Violet was clearing the dinner dishes, my mother presented my father with a book. "Happy birthday," she told him.

"*Pleasant Valley*, by Louis Bromfield," he said with a smile. I crowded close to look at the new book, but it didn't seem very interesting. My mother and father laughed at the cover painting, an artless depiction of a midwestern farm by someone who had obviously never seen one.

"You're really eager to get back to Missouri, aren't you?" my father told my mother.

She nodded. "Yes. I love Lebanon, and all we've seen and done in this year, but I want to have a garden of my own, a home of my own."

My father smiled and closed the book. "The farm in Columbia."

My mother nodded.

"Maybe we bought the farm too soon," my father said. "I still need to work for a while, back in Dhahran."

"We can make it work," my mother told him. "I can stay at the farm in Columbia, start making it into a home. You work in Dhahran and come back to Columbia twice a year on vacations."

He nodded, but he didn't seem happy about it.

Violet came in to say she was leaving for the night.

My mother saw her out then returned to the living room.

"Have you told her we're leaving?" my father asked.

"Not yet," my mother said. "Tomorrow. But I think somehow she already knows."

"I hate to leave," my father said. "After all the work we've put into the training center." He looked somber. "But we don't have any choice. The company is going to close down this operation."

He turned his new book over and over in his hands.

My mother put her hands over his.

"Yes. I know, but all overseas assignments end."

"And a partnership with AUB," my father said. "It could have been world-class." He put a smile on his face. "But, as you said, all overseas assignments end."

Mother smiled and kissed his cheek. "It will work out fine, you'll see."

My father turned to me, "You'll be going to a one-room school there."

I nodded, unsurprised. I was attending a one-room school here, so I assumed one school was much like another. My father glanced at my mother. "The kids will all speak English there. Kind of."

They laughed and I wondered what was so funny.

This was the first I had heard that we'd soon be leaving Sidon. It did not trouble me. I had left Dhahran to move to Kansas City. I had left Kansas City to move to Sidon. I was not concerned about leaving Sidon to move to Columbia.

I saw Karl-Ivar for the last time at the end of my last day at the Sidon school. We awkwardly said goodbye, then I got into the school bus station wagon, in my usual seat. Karl was waiting for his father to pick him up. I waved to Karl as the bus pulled away, and he waved back.

It was not painful.

I knew with inarticulate confidence that I would make new friends at my next school.

My parents spoke of "going home," but for me, and for my sister, home was Dhahran. Moving to Columbia was just moving to another place we had never been before.

The day before we were to leave Sidon, Mother gave Violet her Victrola record player and all ten of her records. Violet thanked her, then finished washing the dishes, hung the towels out to dry on the balcony rail, and gathered up the little suitcase record player and bundle of records. My mother was waiting at the door. They both cried a little but did not hug each other since that is not a Lebanese custom.

My last sight of Violet was of her walking briskly down the road with the little record player and bundle of records.

The next morning, December 14, 1956, we packed our things into six suitcases. All our Lebanon souvenirs and household goods had already been packed into boxes, which would be shipped to the States.

We walked out of Couzhou Beit for the last time, my father closed the wrought iron gates behind us, and Sayeed drove us to the Beirut airport.

The ARAMCO DC-7 departed right on time, bound for Athens, Geneva, Shannon (Ireland), and New York. The plane circled past the cedar-covered mountains and over downtown Beirut. I could make out the long boulevards lined with mimosa trees, the curving Corniche, its row of white and pink hotels gleaming in the morning sun, the cerulean Mediterranean before them.

The coast disappeared into the mist and there was only the deepening blue of the sea. I resumed thinking about a story that was running in my imagination. It was a free-form adventure set on an alien planet, combining ancient Roman ruins, Jules Verne technology, and *Flash Gordon* costumes.

I have never been back to Lebanon. War came in 1995 and lasted until 2010. And so the beautiful Beirut I knew disappeared into history just as surely as the desert city of Baalbek had disappeared two thousand years ago.

I'm sure that time has taken away the people we knew: Sayeed our driver, Violet our housekeeper, Mrs. Martin my teacher, Mr. Habib at the bookstore, the Bushakras at Eagle's Eyrie, and the TAPline employees that came to our house for dinner parties.

But they still exist in my memory.

Aerial photo of Sidon, June 1956

My mother, Ruth at the front door of Couzhou Beit
1956

Living room and dining room of Couzhou Beit

April 1956

Linden and me in upstairs sitting room at Couzhou Beit

October 1956

Me in upstairs room
Couzhou Beit 1956

Mr. Barakat's shop,
Sidon, June 1956

Schoolbus in front of Couzhou Beit
Sidon, May 1956

Sidon Training Center housing and classroms building

January 1956

Sidon Training Center foreground and refinery background

July 1956

Traffic on the road in front of the STC campus
Beirut, 1956

STC looking east
toward the tank farm

STC campus looking south
toward the refinery

STC tankers off shore

Furniture makers and boat builders
Sidon, 1956

Fishing boat under construction,
Sidon, March 1956

Karl and me at the beach
Sidon, September 1956

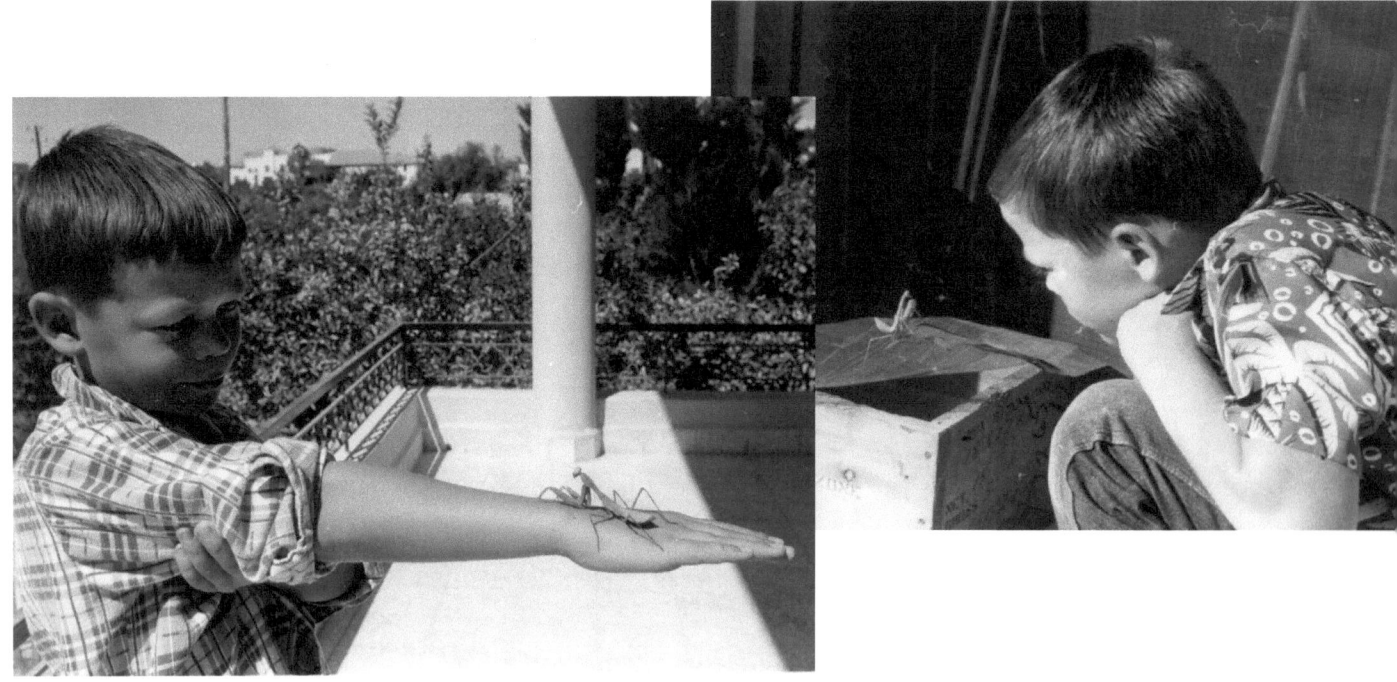

Me with praying mantis on upstairs terrace of Couzhou Beit
Sidon, October 1956

Sidon shore looking south
1956

Earthquake damage
to a house in Sidon
March 1956

Model ship from Sidon

View out the front door of
Couzhou Beit
January 1956

Me at the vegetable stand
Damour, June 1956

The village well in Violet's village

April 1956

Mother, me, and Linden at the Dead Sea

May 1956

Mother and us kids about to enter the Seek

May 1956

Petra, the Seek

May 1956

Linden on horseback
Petra, May 1956

Petra rock colors
May 1956

Me and Linden
Petra, May 1956

The courtyard,
Petra, May 1956

Petra May 1956

Mother, me, and Linden
American Colony Hotel
Garden in Jerusalem
May 1956

Linden and me at the entrance of the American Colony Hotel
Jerusalem, May 1956

Linden and me at the Garden of Gethsemane Jerusalem, May 1956

Me in the Garden of Gethsemane

Me, Linden, and Mother
Bethlehem, May 1956

Walls of Jericho
May 1956

Palm Sunday Route
Jerusalem, May 1956

99

Me, Linden, and Mother
Bethlehem, May 1956

Palm Sunday Route
Jerusalem, May 1956

Mother, Linden, and me
at the Via Dolorosa
Jerusalem, May 1956

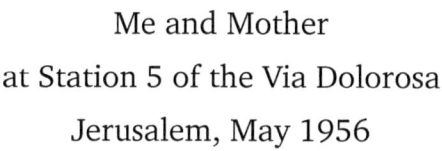

Me and Mother
at Station 5 of the Via Dolorosa
Jerusalem, May 1956

Jerusalem street scene

May 1956

Dome of the Rock mosque from Mount of Olives

Jerusalem, May 1956

St. Georges Hotel
Beirut

Splashing around in the Med
Beirut

Mountain village and terraced fields
Lebanon, 1956

Linden on a horse with Mother at the AUB farm
American University of Beirut

AUB tennis courts
and soccer field
June 1956

Linden on the AUB campus
June 1956

Baalbek, Temple of Jupiter
July 1956

Linden and me at
Baalbek, July 1956

Temple of Jupiter,
Baalbek, July 1956

Lois Luckenbaugh, Linden, me, and Mother
Baalbek, July 1956

Temple of Bacchus
Baalbek
July 1956

Me, Linden, Mother, and Lois Luckenbaugh

Zahle, July 1956

Restaurant in Zahle

July 1956

The road to
Eagle's Eyrie

Mother, Linden, Fuad, me, and Lois Luckenbaugh
Eagle's Eyrie

Mr. and Mrs. Bushakra
Entrance gate to Eagles Eyrie, July 1956

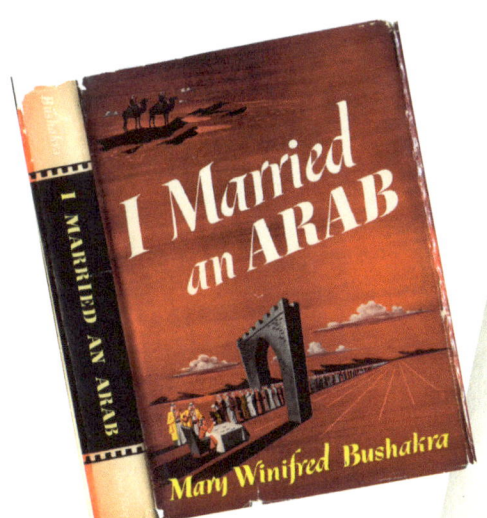

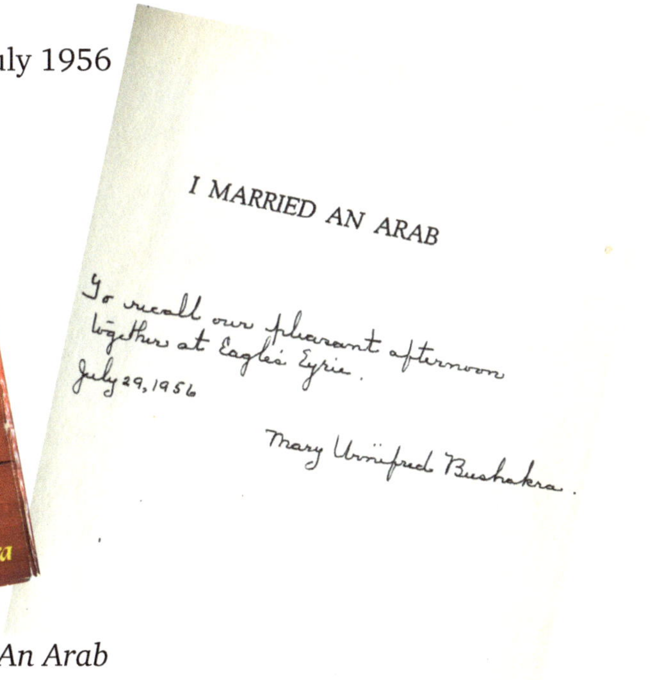

I Married An Arab
Mrs. Bushakra's inscription
and book cover

Mr. and Mrs. Bushakra at Eagles Eyerie

July 1956

The town of Ammatour seen from Eagels Eyerie

July 1956

Tripoli view from hotel window

August 1956

Me and Linden at Tripoli crusader castle

August 1956

Tripoli street scene Linden, me, and Mother

August 1956

Linden with our parents
Byblos, September 1956

Linden on a side street in Byblos September 1956

Ruins at Byblos September 1956

Hotel at Cedars of Lebanon
November 1956

Cedars of Lebanon

Mother, Linden, and Father
Overlook near Cedars of Lebanon
November 1956

Mother, Linden, and me
Cedars of Lebanon
November 1956

Mother, us kids, and friends
Hotel at Cedars of Lebanon, November 1956

Ski lift at
Cedars of Lebanon
November 1956

The big snowstorm at the farm in Columbia
January 1957

Columbia, Missouri, January 1957

I have no memory of our return trip from Lebanon to the USA. I do remember that instead of flying from New York to Kansas City, we flew to St. Louis, where my parents picked up the brand-new blue 1957 Chevrolet station wagon they had ordered. The salesman told my father, "The highway should be clear. We had a heck of a snowstorm two days ago, but the roads are cleared off now. You shouldn't have no trouble getting to KC."

My father had folded down the back seat so we could get all our luggage into the station wagon; my sister and I laid on top of the pile of suitcases. It was fun watching the snow-covered fields flowing by as we drove two-lane Highway 40 from St. Louis to Kansas City.

We spent two days at Grandmother Juna's house in Kansas City then drove to Grandmother Grace's house in Effingham for two days. The coal stove would heat one room nicely, but at bedtime we slid rubber hot-water bottles under the covers before going to bed, then scurried into the freezing cold bedroom and jumped into bed.

During the day I wandered my grandmother's tiny farm, tromping through the snow, daydreaming. It was sparkling white, the air cold and still.

Then my mother and father packed us back into the new station wagon and we drove Highway 40 to Columbia, where we checked into the All States Motel. I thought the motel was cool-looking, a semicircle of little cottages. Number 28 was our own tiny house, with a living room, two bedrooms, a kitchenette, and a bathroom. This would be our home until the Dawsons moved out of the farmhouse and we could move in. I heard my father and mother discussing the last payment on the farm: $9,500.

"And we'll need furniture and linen, pots and pans and plates, lots of stuff," my mother said, her voice edged with concern.

"It will work out fine," my father reassured her.

New Year's Eve we all went to bed early. New Year's Day we watched the Tournament of Roses parade on the little black-and-white TV in the motel living room.

January 2 was cold but sunny. The four of us piled in the station wagon and drove two miles down a gravel road to Valley Springs School. The teacher, Mrs. Dozier, welcomed us and got us seated at our desks.

Strangely, I have no memory of my first day at Valley Springs School.

After dropping my sister and me off at school, my parents returned to the cabin at All States Motel. In his diary my father states that they: *wrote letters, picked up the kids at three PM, bought some food, and ate dinner in our cabin.*

On January 3, while my sister and I were at school, my parents bought beds at Sears and oversaw the delivery of twenty boxes of our belongings to the Dawson farm. My father's diary says: *stored our household things in a shed at the farm. Applied for a phone—$2.97 per month for an eight-party line. The Dawson farm auction was well attended. The livestock sold well, especially hogs. Ruth got a driver's license. We retitled the car in both our names.*

Sunday, January 6, we moved into the Dawson's old house on the farm. The farmhouse was a typical 1940s uninsulated house with a coal furnace, no air-conditioning, and well water. It did have indoor plumbing. (I suspect my mother had laid down the law on that point.) In any case it didn't matter much since they intended to start designing and building a new house as soon as they could find a good architect.

Later in January, it turned colder and very snowy. You had to go outside, around the house, and into the cellar to stoke the old coal-fired furnace. We all missed the big Warm Morning LP gas heater we had had in Lebanon.

Saturday, January 12, my parents conferred with architect Dave Clark about designing a house for them. We all had dinner at the Daniel Boone Hotel restaurant. Then on Thursday, January 17, Dave Clark surveyed our new house location. He and my parents settled on a floor plan for the house.

January 24, 1957, Thursday, Allied Van Lines delivered the last three boxes from Sidon. *Everything we own is now at the farm,* my father wrote in his diary. *No more stored things in Kansas City or overseas.*

My sister and I easily settled into our new school routine. I became accustomed to using an outhouse. I didn't like it but I could do it. Mrs. Dozier helped my sister use the outhouse. At the school in Sidon there had been nice new indoor plumbing. But kids take things in stride.

As winter ended I spent most of my time after school roaming the farm. I really liked being able to roam over many acres of fields and woods. There was a big pond that I planned to swim in when summer came.

My sister and I had identical Dale Evans and Roy Rogers lunchboxes with our names painted on them. I remember one cold winter day, opening my lunchbox and finding warm tomato soup in my thermos. I thought of cold winter evenings in Sidon, the warm LP gas heater running, eating tomato soup with saltines for dinner. For some reason tomato soup seemed like a special treat.

At morning and afternoon recesses we would all bolt from the schoolhouse for our thirty-minute recesses (which Mrs. Dozier would sometimes let stretch to an hour). In front of the school was an open area that the girls used for jump rope or all of us used for softball games. There was a two-swing set on the sloping field beside the schoolhouse, and farther up the grassy slope was an area we used to play "Red Rover." But best of all, across the gravel road was a tiny creek and a tree-covered bluff about fifty feet tall. Trees grew on the many rock ledges. One ledge near the top was what Frank and Sam called their fort. I was soon invited to join them there. "We can set up here and nobody can see us," Frank told me. That seemed important to him.

It didn't take me long to realize that most of my schoolmates had never travelled outside of Missouri. In Sidon most of my schoolmates had travelled all over the world. I also realized I knew the history and geography of the Middle East better than anyone else in the school, including Mrs. Dozier. But I kept my mouth shut so as not to be thought a teacher's pet or a know-it-all.

The spring of 1957—exploring the woods and fields of the farm, reading science fiction books, attending a one-room school where my classmates were congenial and lessons were undemanding—was idyllic.

But those days were not a very good time for my mother. She was forty-five years old, her husband was overseas, she was raising two young kids in an unfamiliar town, living in an old house, and her mother was terminally ill in Kansas City. And most of all she missed the friendships that were so easy to make overseas. I am sure she missed the dinner parties that were a regular event in Sidon. In Columbia there were no dinner parties, no shared experiences, and little opportunity to socialize. But she had met Mrs. Moreau, Daryle Moreau's mother, at the school. Hazel Moreau was very supportive of the school—sort of a one-person PTA. Mrs. Moreau invited my mother to bring my sister and me for a visit one Sunday afternoon.

The Moreaus' house was a short drive from our house. Hazel's husband, Harry Moreau, was owner of a small construction company.

Mr. Moreau was sitting in the living room in sock feet reading the Sunday paper. Mrs. Moreau suggested my sister Linden and her daughter Jill sit out on the shady terrace just outside the windows. "You can show her your dolls, or your 4-H project."

Daryle and I adjourned to his room, where he showed me some model airplanes he had made. I saw a blue corduroy jacket lying on a chair. "Are you in FFA?" I asked.

Daryle said yes, but didn't look too happy about it. "And in 4-H. I'm supposed to be working with my dad on an electrician badge, but he doesn't have much time to help me with it. And this summer I'm going to have even less time since I'll be working for my dad. He's got several houses to get built."

We had a pleasant afternoon talking about this and that—including chess. Daryle had a chess set. He explained the rules to me and we played for a while.

Soon it was time to leave.

Back in Sidon I only had an opportunity to do things with other kids when we would go to the beach, or on a sightseeing excursion with other families. There were no other American kids within walking distance. But here in Columbia, Daryle's farm was within walking distance, and so was Frank Hunt's. At school one day I asked Frank if I could walk over to his house for a visit, but he said I'd better not. His father needed all the Hunt boys to do farm work most days.

A few weeks later I decided to phone Daryle and see if I could come over for a visit. I knew the procedure for using a phone on a party line. First gently pick up the receiver, and if no one was talking, dial the five-digit number.

Daryle answered right away. "Sure, come on over."

I picked up a chess set in a nice leather case that my parents had bought in India and set off across the pasture, past the pond, then into the woods and up the hill to the road. Thirty minutes later I was there. After a few months of roaming around, I knew the woods and fields pretty well.

Mrs. Moreau had made homemade lemonade for us. I found it too sweet, but I drank it anyway.

In Daryle's room we tried to set up the chess pieces, but they were so ornate we couldn't figure what each one was. Soon we closed it up and sat looking through old issues of *Flying* magazine.

"I need to work for my dad this summer, but he said if I saved up some money I could take flying lessons."

That sounded really fun to me.

It was evening by the time I was ready to leave. "Want me to drive you home, young feller?" Mr. Moreau asked.

"No thanks, I'll walk."

"It's getting kind of late . . ."

"I'll walk fast," I told him. I quickly said goodbye and hurried down the road, the gravel scrunching softly under my feet.

I knew I needed to hurry since I'd told my mother I'd be home by dark, and it would be dark soon. At the corner fence of our farm I ducked between the barbed-wire strands and into the woods. It was darker in the woods, but I knew the path quite well.

I had walked for fifteen minutes when I heard a sound, a voice, saying, "Who." Not loud, but very clear. I stood stock-still. The dark woods all around me were silent. Then came another "Who."

I said, "It's me, Mike," and waited for an answer, but there was none. I thought it was probably an owl, but it sounded so human I couldn't be sure. I started trotting down the path as fast as I could, clutching the chess set under my arm. I was glad to reach the end of the woods and start up the open pasture to the house. I told my mother I was sorry I was late, ate the spaghetti dinner she'd made, and went to bed.

With the window open to let in cool night air, and the screen on the window shut tight to keep mosquitos out, I lay perfectly relaxed. The voice in the woods was an owl, I told myself and drifted off to sleep.

Nothing really scary about the owl incident, but I still remember feeling nervous in the darkness and silence of the woods that evening. The owl sounded so human.

Years later I happened across a TV movie called I Heard the Owl Call My Name. *It starred Tom Courtenay as a dying young priest sent to a remote village as his last assignment.*

In Margaret Craven's book the owl is calling Tom to his death and counseling Tom on how to accept death. My owl was only asking me, "Who are you?"

Which is an interesting question. Who was I at age ten and who am I now?

Exploring that question is why I am writing this reminiscence.

Late in the spring, after a big thunderstorm, my mother was driving my sister, me, Frank Hunt, and Daryle Moreau home from school when we found a tree blown down with one limb lying in the gravel road to Frank's house.

"I can move it," Daryle volunteered, and he piled out of the car. "Come on guys." Frank and I followed him out, and it only took a minute for all of us pushing together to shove the limb off into the ditch beside the road. "Frank and I can walk from here," Daryle said. "You all can drive straight ahead on home."

"A very decent boy," my mother said as we drove home.

In those days, in rural Missouri, neighbors always helped each other.

On our frequent weekend trips to Kansas City, while my mother helped Grandmother Juna, I would usually wander up and down Garfield Avenue. The concrete sidewalk was still badly heaved by tree roots. The calls of the blue jays in the big elm trees still sounded as melancholy as they had on my first visit here. This spring most of the trees had a band of some kind of sticky substance around the trunk at the five-foot mark to stop cicadas from crawling up the tree. Some empty shells of cicadas were still stuck in the glue, which I found fascinating.

The house at the farm was not air conditioned, so most nights my mother had a box fan set up in the hallway to circulate air. The springtime insects and frogs were so loud I could hear them at night even with the fan running.

On one of our trips to the library my mother checked out a book about the constellations. It was fun spotting Polaris, the big and little dippers, the Pleiades, and the brighter stars like Sirius and Procyon. I tried to imagine the distance from our solar system to Polaris, but the numbers were so big they were unimaginable. Peering at the stars from my bed, my nose up against the window screen, I could smell the not-unpleasant scent of the wooden screen frame. That smell is what I most remember about that old house.

On our next trip to the library, as I was perusing the bookshelves I came upon the library's small collection of science fiction books. The covers were great—people in spacesuits, fog-shrouded alien planets, spaceships flitting among the stars. I selected a couple of books based on their cover illustrations.

At home I read both of them in three days. Science fiction was the literature for me. From that day forward, that was what I enjoyed reading the most.

My two books had to last two weeks, so I would restrict myself to only reading a few chapters each night in bed. Even so, I often had to reread my books before we made our next trip to the library. Within a few months I had worked through the library's entire selection of science fiction books. There were only about fifty of them.

Although I had read a few books in Lebanon, and my father had read books to us there (I think he read Kon-Tiki to us twice), it was only in Columbia that I began to read books so avidly.

The library had an oak cabinet of little file drawers where each book had a 3x5 card either typed or neatly handwritten with the book title, author name, and Dewey Decimal System number. It was a small library, essentially a single large room, but nicely arranged. And it was air-conditioned, which was not that common in those days. I grew to appreciate that little library. I could wander down the aisles of books glancing at this one and that at random. It was seldom crowded and it had a very comfortable feel to it.

On mild spring days I would wander the fields and woods of the farm and pretend to be in the jungles of Venus or the deserts of Mars. It was wonderful—wandering, daydreaming, examining the incredible complexity of the grasses, the dirt, the bark on giant sycamore trees. Then back to the house for a cold Pepsi over ice in a tall green glass that I favored. My parents only allowed me to have one Pepsi a day, which made it taste even more delicious. Sometimes I'd ask my mother to buy a few bottles of Squirt, the grapefruit-flavored soda, which was almost as good.

May mornings were dew-drenched, the green-gold sunlight streaming across the lawn and the fields. The house was cool, but outside the heat and humidity were already increasing.

Sometimes I would lie in bed and read for a while in the early morning. I remember particularly liking *Plague Ship* and *Sargasso of Space*, both by Andrew North. I read both of them several times.

Andrew North is a pseudonym for Alice Mary Norton, who wrote dozens of quite good science fiction novels in her forty-year career.

There were no childcare facilities in those days, so my mother took my sister and me with her when she went to Safeway for her weekly food shopping. My sister stayed with Mother, but I was allowed to sit on the lower shelf of the magazine rack while she did her shopping. This suited me fine since the science fiction magazines were conveniently (for me) placed on the bottom shelf. There were usually four, sometimes six, different SF magazines on display. I liked *Astounding* the best, but *Amazing* and *Fantastic* were also good. I didn't care much for *Fantasy and Science Fiction* magazine or *Galaxy* magazine.

If I found a particularly good article I could sometimes persuade my mother to buy the magazine for me. I soon had half a dozen magazines at home, which I would read and reread, daydreaming over the Kelly Freas and Van Dongen illustrations.

In one issue of *Astounding Science Fiction* magazine I noticed an advertisement for Doubleday's science fiction book club. I convinced my mother to mail in the $1 fee to join. I got three hardcover books in the mail, and was required to buy two books every month after that at discount prices. They all had BOOK CLUB EDITION stamped on the interior cover jacket flap. But they were well-made books. For my first three books I chose *The Astounding SF Anthology*, Cyril Kornbluth's *A Mile Beyond the Moon*, and *The Omnibus of SF* edited by Groff Conklin.

Daydreamer

I still own all three of them and have reread them multiple times over the years.

That spring my mother planted iris in what had formerly been a large vegetable garden. Before he left to return to work in Dhahran, my father had made arrangements to pay Mr. Morgan, who lived just up the road, to do some farm work for him. So I would often see Mr. Morgan on his old Allis-Chalmers with sickle bar mower, driving down the road to our farm to cut the alfalfa for hay. After Mr. Morgan had finished mowing for the day, I enjoyed walking out and smelling the rich scent of new-mown hay.

The Morgans were our nearest neighbors. Ted Morgan's wife had died several years earlier, and he was left to raise the kids by himself. Bill and Joe, his two eldest sons, had graduated from high school and gone into the military, but that left four girls of various ages still living at home. As was customary in those days, the older girls took care of the younger girls while Mr. Morgan worked seven days a week, dairy farming a dozen cows and row cropping wheat and corn on some rented bottomland. On school days he would drop off all four girls at school, and Mrs. Dozier would drive them home after school.

Janet Morgan told me years later that Mrs. Dozier became a second mother to her. That was one of the strengths of the little one-room country schools. Academics were not great, but the social skills we learned—helping each other, playing together, working together—were priceless.

Despite the demands on his time, Mr. Morgan always managed to get the hay on our property cut and baled and stacked in the hayshed. We did not have a TV set in those days, but the Morgan family did. So many Sunday evenings we would walk down the road to the Morgans' house and watch the Walt Disney show.

Most Sunday afternoons if it was not raining (and sometimes when it was raining), I would roam the fields and the woods, exploring and imagining I was on an alien planet.

The natural world was endlessly fascinating to me then, and still is.

Saturdays we almost always went to town for a visit to the library, then we would walk up Broadway three blocks to J.J. Newberry and F.W. Woolworth before going to Safeway.

In those days the "dime stores" like Newberry's and Woolworth's sold many well-made and useful items, so my mother shopped there often. I liked going to True Value Hardware, which was located between the two dime stores. Inside it was festooned with all kinds of tools and gloves and a cabinet with dozens of little drawers full of various-sized screws and bolts and nails and washers. My mother usually entrusted me to buy what she needed at the hardware store while she and my sister shopped at the bigger stores.

We rendezvoused on the sidewalk in front of Woolworth's.

"What's in the bag?" I asked my mother.

"A record," she said.

We started walking back to the car.

"Remember Violet in Sidon?" she said. "I gave her my records when we left, but I like some of them so bought another copy for our record player."

I assumed it was *My Fair Lady*.

When we got home Mother showed my sister and me her new record, which was a collection of songs by the Fontane Sisters.

I didn't stay around to listen since I was eager to take a quick swim in the pond before dinner.

As I banged out the screen door I heard "Chanson D'Amour" playing on the record player and remembered the little fruit and vegetable stand at the village of Damour on the road from Sidon to Beirut. I still had no idea why someone would sing a song about that village.

Wearing my swimming suit, tee shirt, and sandals I walked to the pond, stripped off my shirt, and waded into the cool silty mud while tiny green frogs leaped into the water.

I could feel the cool water and mud under my feet while the water at the surface was warm. I swam around for a while, then floated on my back. Dragonflies flitted across the water in a flash of iridescence.

I reveled in the sense of stillness, floating on water beneath a cloudless sky.

The Saturday before school ended, Mother took my sister and me to the Western Auto store at the corner of Walnut and Sixth Street. New bikes were hanging in a row by their front wheels from the ceiling along one wall.

My mother asked if they had a twenty-inch bike.

"Smallest we have is twenty-one inches," the crew-cut salesman told her. He waved a dismissive hand at a row of small training bikes. "Except for these kiddie bikes."

"Think he'd be OK on a twenty-one-inch bike?"

The salesman, eager to make a sale, grinned and said, "Sure, just takes a little practice. Kids catch on fast." He used a long wooden pole with a steel hook to bring down a bright-red Western Flyer from the ceiling rack.

It seemed kind of big to me, but I didn't say anything. The salesman held the bike steady between his knees and hoisted me onto the seat. My feet reached the pedals, barely. "You doing OK, Champ?"

I nodded.

"You can't ride it here. Let's take it out to the sidewalk."

I didn't want to risk falling down and having people see me, so I quickly said, "That's OK. This one is good." I liked the fact that it had the kind of brakes that came on when you put backpressure on the pedals, not like the French-made adult bikes in Lebanon, which had handgrips that pressed little pads against the sides of the wheels. My mother paid for the bike, the salesman loaded it into the back of the station wagon, and we went home. I immediately tried riding it up and down the gravel driveway, and it was a little wobbly, but as long as I kept going fairly fast I was OK. I started to get out on the gravel road, but my mother waved me back.

I rode my new bike around the yard, up and down the driveway, and around the flat part of the newly mowed hay field. But it wasn't like Dhahran where I could ride all around the housing compound on the empty streets. I liked having a bike again, with the sense of freedom it provided, but it was not as much fun as I remembered it to be.

I put the bike in the shed and sat on the front steps of the house in the shade. I thought about taking the garden hose and making a river system like Jim McGruder and I had done in the sandy backyard at Dhahran, but it didn't seem that interesting now. Eventually I wandered back into the house and lay on my bed reading another chapter in *Islands in the Sky* by Arthur C. Clarke.

Sunday I read some more and then went out into the glaring summer sun and across the mown hay into the cool woods. The forest floor was dappled by light coming through the leaves of the giant sycamore trees.

The last three days of school were almost entirely unstructured. Recesses lengthened to an hour. All of us, Mrs. Dozier included, were glad to get out of the stifling schoolhouse for a while. Inside, I spent most of the last days reading through the stack of old *National Geographic* magazines that had been donated to the school. Once I found an article about the Swiss Alps, with a photo of the Matterhorn and of Zermatt village, and daydreamed for a time about our Christmas holiday there, the scent of cut firewood and the fresh pine Christmas tree in the dining room. And the thrill of sliding down the white snow on skis.

On the last day of school, at morning recess, Frank and Sammy and I clambered across the little creek (it had rained in the night) and up the rocky path to our fort. The air was heavy with moisture evaporating under a bright sun. But there were low clouds in the west, which I had learned meant more rain was coming.

"Where did you move here from?" I asked Sammy.

Sammy was systematically putting a twig in the path of an ant. The ant would climb over it or go around it and Sammy would then move the twig in front of the ant again. "We used to live in Illinois (pronouncing it ell-uh-noise) a long time ago. I don't remember it."

"Are you going to move again?" I asked.

He studied the ant, placed the twig again. "I don't know. We'll move if my dad needs to find work I guess. Why?"

Daydreamer

"I always lived here," Frank said. "Why would you move?"

I shrugged. Moving was a way of life for me. We moved because my parents said we were moving.

"What are you going to do this summer?" Sammy asked.

"Work for my dad, same as always," Frank said.

"My mom said we may not go to the lake this summer," Sammy said. "We ain't got enough money, my mom says. My dad was going to take me fishing. He likes to fish and drink Falstaff. He fell out of the boat one time last summer. Got pretty mad when we laughed."

"I think we should get back together again sometime in the future," I said. "Years in the future."

"What for?" Frank asked. "We'll see each other next year at the new school."

"I mean years from now, when we're teenagers. So we can meet up and see what became of each other." This was a novel thought for me. Up until now my friendships only lasted a year or two.

I took out the pocketknife I had started carrying and opened the second-biggest blade and picked some gray lichen off a rock. It was a beautiful striated gray.

"We'd be the same," Sammy said, disinterested in my idea. "Why would we change?"

"People change as they get old," Frank said. "I see my older brothers changing."

We sat there for a while, not speaking. The wind was hot, coming in off the hayfield where the bales lay in the sun, but there were occasional cool breezes from the approaching rain clouds. Under the tree it was cool. A cricket chirred. We could see Mrs. Dozier walking around the schoolhouse, shaking her head at the damage deer had done to her day lilies.

I wondered if there would be a closing ritual today. I had grown accustomed to the daily ritual at Valley Springs School. Pledge allegiance to the flag, then two of the boys would take the flag outside and run it up the flagpole. Then before we started our lessons we'd chant the names of the books of the Bible in order from Genesis to Revelation. That litany had become so ingrained in my memory that I'd often hear it running through my head while we played softball or looked for tadpoles in the creek or climbed the little bluff above the creek.

Frank was mumbling that litany now. ". . . first and second Kings, first and second Samuel . . ."

Sammy picked up the chant ". . . first and second Chronicles, Ezra, Nehi, Esther, Job. . ."

"I wonder if Nehi Cola is named after that book of the Bible?" Frank speculated.

"Nope," Sammy stated authoritatively. "They can't put names from the Bible on stuff for sale."

"I like the cherry Nehi," Frank said. "The pop machine in front of the store in Huntsdale has them."

The school bell rang and we started down the path from the bluff. In my mind's eye I could see the dusty ruin of the Roman city of Baalbek where we'd driven one Saturday. The white limestone blocks forming the base of the forum, the row of Corinthian columns, the outlines of stone foundations under a hot desert sun, silent in the desert wind. It was hot after the cool breeze from the Mediterranean back in Sidon. I knew that the ruins of Baalbek were still standing, back in Lebanon, on the other side of the world. I thought maybe I would go back there sometime.

Mrs. Dozier had our graduation certificates ready for us, saying we'd all successfully passed. After she'd inspected each of our textbooks and had us stack them in order in the storage cabinet in the back of the room, she dismissed school for the last time. We grabbed our lunchboxes and hurried out to the road, waving goodbye. Sammy went south, Frank and I and my sister turned north. The road was very muddy, but we hardly noticed.

That day the hundred-year history of one-room rural schools in mid-Missouri ended. A brand-new consolidated elementary school had been built, and the next fall, school buses would pick kids up and take them home. The new school had clean indoor bathrooms, good heat, good light, new desks, and cafeteria lunches—all positive changes. But it did not have the sense of community that the one-room schools did. For a century these tiny schools had sprung up whenever and wherever a community found they had enough children to warrant building a building and hiring a teacher. The local farm families did all the school maintenance and repairs. When books or supplies were needed, the farmers' wives would collect money and buy what was needed.

Now that was over.

A tiny article in the back pages of the Columbia Daily Tribune *newspaper in December 1957 noted that the Valley Springs School building had sold for $50 to a farmer who planned to use it as a hay storage shed.*

Today there is no trace of Valley Springs School.

I woke early in the morning on the first day of summer vacation and lay in bed listening to robins and bluebirds and a distant blue jay.

After a time I got out of bed and dressed. My two library books lay on the chair, their imaginary worlds tugging at my imagination. The house was silent. I padded out onto the porch and down the four concrete steps to the dusty ground. The ground was cool on my bare feet. Around the corner I watched the sun edge above the horizon, shading from red to pale gold in the humid air.

Summer vacation stretched out before me with limitless possibilities.

View of the house, 1957

Box of household goods and souvenirs

Sidon to Columbia

Looking north from the farmhouse

Spring 1957

Me and Linden in the shade at the old house
1958

Linden, Grandmother Juna, and me (with terrapin)
on our way to church
Spring 1957

The last day of school at Valley Springs School

May 1957

Linden walking home from school with lunchboxes

May 1957

Linden and me — Summer of 1957
Columbia, Missouri

www.ingramcontent.com/pod-product-compliance
Lightning Source LLC
Chambersburg PA
CBHW041535220426
43663CB00002B/40